A CHRISTIAN WRITER'S
MANUAL
OF STYLE

A CHRISTIAN WRITER'S
MANUAL
OF STYLE

edited by
Bob Hudson
and Shelley Townsend

ZONDERVAN PUBLISHING HOUSE
GRAND RAPIDS, MICHIGAN

A CHRISTIAN WRITER'S MANUAL OF STYLE
Copyright © 1988 by the Zondervan Corporation

Zondervan Books
are published by Zondervan Publishing House
1415 Lake Drive, S.E.
Grand Rapids, MI 49506

Library of Congress Cataloging-in-Publication Data

A Christian writer's manual of style.

   Includes indexes.
   1. Christian literature—Authorship. 2. Authorship—Style manuals. I.
Hudson, Bob, 1953– . II. Townsend, Shelley, 1954– .
BR44.C48 1988   808'.02   88-20612
ISBN 0-310-35021-2

Unless otherwise noted, all Scripture references are taken from the *Holy Bible: New International Version* (North American Edition), copyright © 1973, 1978, 1984 by the International Bible Society. Used by permission of Zondervan Bible Publishers.

Printed in the United States of America

88 89 90 91 92 93 94 / PP / 10 9 8 7 6 5 4 3 2 1

Contents

Preface

"Like a game, language is limited by its rules," wrote linguist Joseph Shipley. On the surface, *A Christian Writer's Manual of Style* appears to be a rule book, for it outlines a practical editorial standard for writers, editors, and proofreaders of religious books. But it also acknowledges that the rules of written language are formulated not by manuals, but by writers.

This book attempts to define a common style, a utilitarian style used by religious writers in the United States and understood by their readers. Where confusion exists, this manual becomes didactic; it becomes a rule book. The rules are not inviolable, but merely techniques of avoiding certain problems so the game of writing may run more smoothly.

But why a Christian manual of style? Or as humorist Artemus Ward once asked, "Why care for grammar as long as we are good?"

One reason is that words have special significance for the Christian. God spoke his creation into being and wrote his laws on stone. Scripture itself is called "the Word," and Christ is referred to as "the Word Incarnate." The earliest printed books in most Western languages were Bibles, and the words of Scripture have shaped our civilization.

Christians owe it to themselves to be conscious of their words; they are full of history and power and spiritual significance. This manual encourages Christians who work professionally with words to become more aware of the nuances of the language and how those words go together.

Another answer to Artemus Ward's question is best summarized by G. K. Chesterton. Although he was referring to spelling, the thought is as true of grammar, punctuation, and usage: "If you spell a word wrong you have some temptation to think it wrong." Christians need right words every bit as much as right thinking for their message to be effective.

Finally, because of the special character of Christian publishing, a different stylistic emphasis is often required, and many questions arise that cannot be answered in the standard references. *Webster's Third New International Dictionary*, along with its abridgment, *Webster's Ninth New Collegiate Dictionary*, are our authorities for spelling and usage. Many of the style points in this manual are similar to those set forth in *The Chicago Manual of Style* (13th edition),* published by the University of Chicago Press (a helpful addition, by the way, to the library of any author, editor, or proofreader). Although compatible with these resources, this manual deviates from them in many significant ways.

This guide has been compiled with an abiding respect for the literary functions of English and a sensitive awareness to the special needs of Christians who work with words. In giving careful attention to these mechanical aspects of the language, authors, editors, and proofreaders alike will build a foundation for producing works of increasingly better quality.

---

*Note: In the following pages we often refer to *The Chicago Manual of Style* by its common abbreviation, CMS.

Acknowledgments

Much of this book is a revision of the second edition of *The Zondervan Manual of Style*, published in 1980. Although many additions and changes have gone into *A Christian Writer's Manual of Style*, the true authors of this book are the editors and former editors of Zondervan Publishing House. Special thanks to: Mary Bombara, Nelle Brinks, Al Bryant, Linda DeVries, Paul Hillman, John Iwema, Judith Markham, Becky Omdahl, Louise Rock, Jim Ruark, Gerard Terpstra, and Ed Viening. This book is largely the product of their labors.

We also wish to thank the advisory committee: Joe Allison, Stan Gundry, Paul Hillman, and Randy Tucker.

A large group of contributors, advisers, and encouragers should be noted and thanked: Phil Bandy; Louise Bauer, the project's designer; Jean Bloom, who organized the proofreading; Cheryl Forbes, who initiated the revision; Len Goss, who shared the resources of his library; Sue Hall; Tammy Johnson, who did the interior layout; Doug Johnston; Nia Jones, who typed the manuscript; Dave Lambert; Julie Link; Mary McCormick; Jan Ortiz; Jon Petersen; Dallas Richards; Judy Schafer, the project's typesetter; John Sloan; Michael Smith; Larry Taylor, who designed the cover; Ed van der Maas; Sandy Vander Zicht, who made many valuable suggestions; Paul Van Duinen; Lori Walburg; and Bob Wood. Credit also goes to the proofreaders: Diane Bloem, Marsha Hoffman, Ruth Naylor, and Mary Ann Pickell.

And finally we wish to thank the reviewing editors for their many revisions and suggestions: Martha Manikas-Foster and Jim Ruark. Their expertise can be found on every page of this book.

I.
FROM MANUSCRIPT
TO BOOK

A. Manuscript Preparation

1. A manuscript prepared for a publisher should be typed on one side only of standard 8½-by-11-inch white bond paper, double-spaced, with at least a one-inch margin on all sides. Colored papers, thin papers (such as onion skin), and erasable-bond papers are unacceptable. No staples, binders, or paper clips should be attached to any portion of the manuscript. When typed on a word processor, the manuscript should be printed, if at all possible, on a letter-quality printer and on standard paper or on continuous-feed paper perforated to convert to standard paper. Extra-wide or lined computer papers are not acceptable.

2. Some publishers require the author to provide two copies of a manuscript, one for editing and typesetting and the other for review, cost estimates, and design. Other publishers request only one copy that is clean enough for photocopying; that is, it should be in dark type, with no cut-and-paste material that might jam a copier, and with all handwritten additions in black ink (not blue). In all cases, the author should be sure to retain a copy of the manuscript.

3. Pages should be numbered consecutively throughout the book, rather than beginning each chapter with page 1.

Numbering may begin with the body of the book or with the front matter. If an author's word processor does not allow for the consecutive numbering of all the pages of an entire manuscript, then the pages should be numbered by hand in the upper right-hand corners. Page numbers are usually circled to distinguish them from other numbers that might appear near the top of each page.

4. Notes, whether intended to be set as footnotes or placed at the end of the chapter or book, should be typed together in a separate section at the end of the manuscript.

5. The author is responsible for providing a clear and readable manuscript, communicating to the editor all matters of preference (especially when they conflict with the publisher's accepted style) and distinctive features of the manuscript preparation that may require the editor's special attention. General responsibilities in regard to obtaining permissions to quote published sources, accuracy of quoted material, complete and detailed references, and other matters are delineated in this manual, but before submitting a manuscript the author should be familiar with any additional requirements specified by the publisher.

6. The author is responsible for checking the accuracy of all Scripture references and the wording of quotations from Scripture before submitting the manuscript to the publisher. The author should also indicate the Scripture version used and inform the editor if a personal translation or paraphrase has been used. When no translation is preferred, this manual recommends *The New International Version* as an accurate and accessible modern translation.

7. Since religious books often contain words or quotations from languages, such as Greek and Hebrew, whose characters are not ordinarily found on the average typewriter or word processor, the author is responsible for

clearly hand-rendering such characters and any accompanying diacritical marks in their correct positions. Since some photocopy machines may blur hand-written characters, the author should send the hand-rendered original to the publisher and keep the copy. In many cases, transliteration may be preferable. A list of Greek and Hebrew transliterations is shown on pages 84–85.

8. Authors should make a conscious effort to eliminate sexist bias in their language. Such bias is often unintentional and taken for granted, and much of it rests on the use of anachronistic forms, obsolete terms, stereotyped gender assumptions, and unnecessary labeling. Guidelines and examples are found in section IV.I.

B. Front Matter

1. The preliminary elements of any book should be arranged in the following order, as appropriate:

    Half title
    Frontispiece or list of other books by same author or in same series
    Title page
    Copyright page
    Dedication
    Epigraph (if it applies to entire book)
    Contents
    List(s) of maps, illustrations, or charts
    List of abbreviations
    Foreword
    Preface
    Acknowledgments
    Introduction
    Inside half title

2. Due to space considerations in some books, half-title pages may be dropped altogether. In some reprints the half-title page may be replaced to make room for quotations from reviews, descriptive copy of the book, or an author's biography.

3. The copyright page, which is prepared by the publisher, includes the official copyright notice, with the date and the copyright holder; Library of Congress Cataloging-in-Publication Data (for library classification); an International Standard Book Number (ISBN), which is a coding system used worldwide; credits and permissions; disclaimers and other brief notes from the editor or author; a brief printing and publishing history of the volume; edition and printing reference numbers; and other information deemed necessary by the publisher.

4. The words *dedication* or *dedicated to* should not be used in the dedication itself, nor is it necessary to use the heading "Dedication."

5. Generally, a foreword is written by someone other than the author. A preface, however, is written by the author. It is not necessary to sign the author's name to the preface if its authorship is clear. If two or more prefaces are reprinted from various editions of the book, the preface for the most recent edition should appear first, followed by the next most recent, and so on. The original preface should appear closest to the text itself. The same rule applies to forewords and introductions.

C. Text

1. The elements of a part and chapter of any book should be arranged in the following order, as appropriate:

    Part-title page
    Part epigraph (if it applies to entire part)
    Chapter-title page
    Chapter epigraph (if it applies to chapter only)
    Chapter number and title
    Text of chapter
    Discussion questions
    Chapter endnotes
    Chapter bibliography or "For Further Reading"

2. In print, the first chapter of the book should begin on a *recto* (right-hand) page. Recto pages have odd numbers and *verso* (left-hand) pages have even numbers. Subsequent chapters may begin on either recto or verso pages, depending on the design and available space.

3. Generally, part- and chapter-title pages are placed on unnumbered recto pages. When these special title pages are used, the table of contents should list the page number on which the actual text of that part or chapter begins, not the number that would have appeared on the part- or chapter-title page.

4. Traditionally running heads display the book title on the verso pages and the chapter title on the recto pages, though this format is less common than it once was. Any number of combinations of book title, chapter title, part title, section heads, author name(s), and other elements may be used in the running heads. They are frequently dropped altogether in popular fiction and mass market books. Page numbers (called *folios*) may appear on the same line as the running heads or separately. The format for the running heads is up to the editor's and designer's discretion.

5. In the manuscript the author should clearly indicate the placement of photos, diagrams, tables, and other graphic material. Valuable photographs or other documents should not be submitted with the manuscript. Photocopies will suffice until such time as the publisher needs to reproduce the originals.

6. In typing the manuscript, the author should use a consistent method of distinguishing various levels of subheadings. In a book with three levels of subheads, for instance, the author might type the A-level heads in all caps, the B-level heads in caps and lowercase, and the C-level heads underlined and run into the text. For disk-submitted manuscripts, however, see special format considerations on pages 158–61.

D. Back Matter

1. Back matter should normally be arranged in the following order, as appropriate:

   Appendix(es)
   Study questions (if not incorporated into the text)
   Notes (if not placed as footnotes or as chapter endnotes)
   Glossary
   Chronological table(s)
   Bibliography or "For Further Reading"
   Index to maps
   Proper-name index
   Subject index
   Scripture index
   Author biographical note
   Colophon

2. When called for in a manuscript, indexes are usually prepared by the author, who will be furnished page proofs by the editor. (A discussion of indexes begins on page 138. For a thorough review of techniques of compiling indexes, authors are referred to chapter 18 of *The Chicago Manual of Style* [CMS].)

3. A colophon is a short notice on the last page of a book in which the publisher can describe the typefaces used in the book, the equipment used, the printer, and any other information related to the production of the book.

E. Rights and Permissions

1. It is the publisher's responsibility to apply for and secure proper copyright for new publications, and the publisher also retains the privilege of granting permission for the reprinting of excerpts as requested for use in other publications.

2. It is the author's responsibility to obtain permission for quoting or copying from other published works, whether poems, songs, interviews, illustrations, cartoons, record-

ings, unpublished dissertations, lectures and speeches, or textual matter. *The Literary Market Place*, available at most libraries, is an excellent resource for finding publishers' addresses for permission purposes.

When writing for permission to quote from a printed source, the author should provide the publisher of the quoted material the following information: the title and author(s) of the work from which the quote will be taken; a description or copy of the material to be quoted, along with an explanation of how the quotation will be used; an approximate total of the number of words to be quoted; the title and author(s) of the work in which the quote will be used; the projected publication date; the number of copies in the first print run; the projected retail price; a one-sentence synopsis of the work's subject.

The author should request "nonexclusive world rights for all editions in all languages," since the author's work may eventually be reprinted in other languages and other editions. Although the granting publisher may limit the rights only to a specific edition or in a given language or country, it is best to try to obtain the broadest possible rights. Whenever possible, permissions should be obtained before the final manuscript is given to an editor. All fees for permissions are to be paid by the author and may be deducted from royalties by arrangement with the publisher.

3. If numerous permissions are required, authors may group the permission notices together in an acknowledgments section. Permission notices, whether grouped together or given individually, should exactly follow any special wording required by the permission grantor.

4. The common-law doctrine of "fair use" permits an author under some circumstances to quote from other works without going through the formalities of requesting permission. In most cases, it is safe to quote up to a total of three hundred words from a book without seeking permission, although citations from shorter works, such

as magazine articles, should be kept proportionately shorter.

5. All copyrighted poems, song lyrics, or parts of poems or lyrics require reprint permission. Works in the public domain do not require permission; these are works not now under copyright either because the copyright time limit has expired or because they preceded copyright legislation. As of January 1, 1978, the term of copyright under normal conditions extends for fifty years after the author's death.

6. Frequent or extended use of passages from modern Scripture versions or translations generally requires permission.

7. Even quotations for which permission is not needed should be given proper credit in notes, on the copyright page, or in the acknowledgments.

F. Proofs

For a more detailed description of proof-handling procedures, see chapter IX.

1. An edited manuscript passes through several stages in the production process: design and sample pages, typesetting, first proofs, second or final proofs, camera copy, plate-making, press, and binding.

2. Customarily the editor will furnish the author with a set of first proofs (the first typesetting run) and indicate a deadline for returning them. Extensive or frequent revisions at this stage are costly, and as stipulated in the author's contract, these costs may be charged to the author if they exceed stated limits. If an editor or author expects many revisions in a manuscript and if time permits, the editor might consider sending the author the edited manuscript (if the book is edited on paper) or a

computer print-out of the edited manuscript (if edited on a word processor) before the first proofs are run.

3. Authors who have been furnished first proofs will receive second or final proofs *only* if the book calls for an index. In this case, authors will be given a deadline by which to complete their compilation of the index. Manuscript revisions (other than the correction of typographical errors) are not permitted at this stage.

II.
PUNCTUATION

This manual does not attempt to cover every rule or problem in the use of punctuation, only those most frequently encountered in writing and editing, and those that have special application to religious publishing. Additional instruction and illustrations can be found in *The Chicago Manual of Style* (CMS), *Words Into Type*, or any up to date grammar or handbook of the English language.

A. Period

1. The period commonly indicates the end of a declarative or imperative sentence.

2. The period is often used for initials and abbreviations, although some abbreviations do not use periods. (See rules for abbreviations in chapter VI.)

   | J. I. Packer | B.C.P. | OT |
   | M.Div. | 1 Thess. | FDR |

3. When items are listed vertically, a period should follow the numbers or letters.

   1. Susanna Wesley
   2. Hannah More
   3. Phoebe Palmer

4. In a vertical list, a period is used after each item only if at least one of the items is a complete sentence.

Among Whitefield's favorite themes were the following:

1. God's love is boundless.
2. Man is miserable without God.
3. Repentance is necessary for salvation.

5. No period should follow titles, running heads, display type, bylines, chapter heads, or subheads that are set off from the text. When a sublevel head is run into the text, however, it should be followed by a period.

6. With photo captions and other descriptive copy attached to charts or graphic illustrations, a period is used only when such copy forms a complete sentence.

Illustration: Thomas Cromwell

Table 1: This chart traces the evolution of the reprints of the King James Version.

B. Comma

1. A comma is placed before a coordinating conjunction (such as *and, but, or, nor, for*) in a compound sentence. No comma is needed when both clauses of the compound sentence are fairly short. When one or both of the clauses are long or contain internal punctuation, a semicolon should be used before the conjunction in place of the comma. Bear in mind, however, that a compound sentence differs from a sentence with a compound predicate (that is, two or more verbs with the same subject), in which case a comma should not be used.

True Christian love can sometimes get angry, but it is also constantly wary of anger's pitfalls.
We seek a human Christ but we also seek a transcendent Christ.
The pagan philosophers gave many admirable precepts, both for resigning blessings and sustaining misfortunes; but lacking the

motives and sanctions of Christianity, however, they produce
little practical effect.—Hannah More
God teaches us patience and produces in us whatever other virtues
we may exhibit.

2. Commas should not be used to set off adjectival clauses or
    phrases that restrict the meaning of the noun they
    modify. Commas should be used, though, when the
    phrase or clause does not strictly identify (restrict) the
    noun. The most common rule of thumb states that when
    the modifying phrase could be eliminated without chang-
    ing the basic meaning of the sentence, then commas
    should be used.

    The translation proposed to King James I in 1604 became known as
        the Authorized Version. [The phrase "proposed to King James I
        in 1604" restricts the noun.]
    This version, translated from the original languages, was not
        printed until 1611. ["translated from the original languages"
        does not restrict the noun.]

3. When a word or phrase is placed in apposition to a noun,
    it is set off by commas. If the word or phrase is restrictive,
    however, no commas should be used. Again, the best rule
    of thumb is that when the word or phrase can be
    eliminated without changing the basic meaning of the
    sentence, commas should be used.

    John Wycliffe, the fourteenth-century reformer, has been called
        "the Morning Star of the Reformation."
    her husband, Robert Pearsall Smith
    his brother, Charles [indicates that Charles is the only brother]
    his brother Charles [indicates that there is more than one brother]
    the poet Milton
    the short story "Revelation" by Flannery O'Connor

4. A comma is placed before *and*, *or*, and *nor* connecting the
    last two elements in a series of three or more. This is
    known as the *serial comma*. Also, set off *etc.*, *namely*, *i.e.*,
    or similar elements with commas.

Both John and Charles Wesley were prolific writers of letters, journals, sermons, and hymns.

She wrote her thesis on the major English mystics, namely, Richard Rolle, Walter Hilton, and Julian of Norwich.

5. A comma usually follows a dependent clause (either restrictive or nonrestrictive) when that clause comes before the main clause of the sentence. A comma is also used before nonrestrictive dependent clauses that follow the main clause. A comma should not be used, however, when a restrictive dependent clause follows the main clause.

Although Merton entered the monastery in 1941, he continued to write poetry throughout his life.

Galileo finally agreed to recant, although he was rumored to have recanted his recantation.

Dorothy Sayers was not allowed to graduate after earning her "first" at Oxford.

6. When an adverbial phrase comes before the main clause of the sentence, the phrase is followed by a comma, although it may be omitted when the phrase is short and when the omission will not result in confusion. The comma should also be omitted when the introductory adverbial phrase is immediately followed by the verb it modifies.

Not many years after surviving a storm at sea, John Newton committed his life to Christ.

After the decree Latimer was free to preach anywhere in England.

Two years before, his ministry had ended. [Were the comma omitted, misreading might result.]

On the altar stood the completed carving of the nativity.

7. Two or more adjectives in sequence should be separated by a comma (or commas) when each, by itself, modifies the noun—that is, if *and* could be inserted between them without changing the basic meaning of the phrase. If an adjective, however, modifies both a subsequent adjective

(or adjectives) and the noun, a comma should not be used.

Margaret Fell proved to be a faithful, sincere friend.
Caedmon was the first great devotional poet to write in English.

8. A comma should be placed between unrelated numerals, although rewriting is often the best way to deal with such situations. A comma should also be used when confusion would result from the juxtaposition of two unrelated proper names or when a word is juxtaposed to itself.

In August of 1670, 450 people heard William Penn preach in front of his padlocked church. [original]
In August of 1670, William Penn preached to 450 people in front of his padlocked church. [rewritten]
For Walton, Donne was the premier poet of his day.
His theology seemed to echo Pope's opinion that whatever is, is right.

9. In some cases a comma may indicate that a word or phrase has been dropped. If the meaning is clear without it, the comma is not necessary.

Newman contributed twenty-four tracts to the series; Keble, nine; and Pusey, four.
We know that the Corinthians received at least two letters from Paul, and the Ephesians one.

10. Commas may be used to set off quotations or sayings, whether or not quotation marks are used. If the quotation is long or formal, a colon should be used in place of the comma. When the entire quotation is used as though it were a noun (for instance, as a subject of a sentence or as a predicate nominative), it should not be set off by commas.

He said, "The world God loves is the world he sees in his only begotten son."
He was fond of the old saw, Too heavenly minded to be any earthly good.
"I forgive you" is a primary assertion of the Christian life.

11. Use a comma after *oh* when other words follow it, but not after the vocative O. Some phrases, such as *oh yes* and *oh no*, are so common, particularly in dialogue, that the comma is not used after *oh* in these combinations.

Oh, Jerusalem!
O mighty king!
He sang, "Oh yes! I belong to the band! Hallelu!"

12. Adverbs, interjections, and other similar words should be set off by commas when they interrupt the flow of thought. Commas are not necessary, however, when these words do not disrupt the continuity.

Margery Kempe, obviously enough, was too impulsive to attract disciples.
The sincerity of Constantine's faith, alas, has often been questioned.
Eventually Cowper contributed to the *Olney Collection*.
"Sinners in the Hands of an Angry God" was indeed Edwards' most famous sermon.

C. Semicolon

1. A semicolon is used in the place of a conjunction between two independent clauses of a compound sentence. Such words as *then, however, thus, hence, indeed, therefore, moreover, consequently, also, yet,* and *so* are thought of as transitional adverbs, not conjunctions, when they are used between independent clauses; therefore, such a word is preceded by a semicolon.

Mary Slessor knew the hardships of the mission field; she would have been appalled by the romantic image that eventually surrounded her work.
Wilberforce thought of himself as a Christian above all else; moreover, he saw his abolitionist views as an outgrowth of his faith.

2. In lists of Scripture references, a semicolon should be placed between separate chapter references or chapter-

and-verse references. Verse references within chapters should be separated by commas.

> He noted the following: Luke 1:46–55; 2:14; and Acts 1:7–8.
> The readings for the morning were John 1:1–13, 15, and 29–34.

3. When items enumerated in running text are particularly long or contain internal punctuation, semicolons should be substituted for commas in those cases when commas alone would not clarify the relationship of one item to another.

> Hannah More knew many of the famous people of her day: Samuel Johnson; Horace Walpole; David Garrick, who produced her plays; William Wilberforce, the abolitionist politician; and John Newton, who eventually became a major influence in her life.

4. Before such expressions as *that is, namely, i.e.,* and *e.g.,* a semicolon may be used, depending on the context and the degree to which the continuity of thought is interrupted. Note, however, that the use of scholarly abbreviations such as *i.e.* and *e.g.* is now generally discouraged in nonacademic writing.

> Lewis wrote Greeves that he had crossed a major threshold in his life; that is, he had passed from "believing in God to definitely believing in Christ."
> These hymnals, e.g., *The Sacred Harp* and its imitators, flourished throughout the South.

D. Colon

1. A colon acts as a pointer to something that follows a particular word, phrase, or sentence. It can introduce a question, quotation, example, or amplification. It may act as a substitute for such expressions as *that is, namely, for instance,* and *for example.* Today a semicolon is used more often than a colon between two closely related sentences.

> That is what faith is: God perceived intuitively by the heart, not by reason.—Pascal

Remember the words of Augustine: "Hasten more slowly."

Many writers shaped the genre of prison literature: Paul, Boethius, and Bunyan.

It was the golden age of revivalism: Moody, Torrey, and Sunday were the familiar names of the time.

It was the golden age of revivalism; Moody, Torrey, and Sunday were the familiar names of the time. [with semicolon]

2. A colon may introduce a direct quotation when no verb-of-saying is used.

Luther's answer was unapologetic: "Here I stand; I cannot do otherwise."

3. Use a colon when quoted material or a list is placed in a separate paragraph after an introductory statement. An introductory statement should not be followed by a colon if the series completes the sentence.

Consider this passage from Arthur Dent's *Plain Man's Pathway to Heaven*: [. . .]

The three areas of Tolkien studies are
1. The works of fantasy
2. The literary criticism
3. The personal writings

4. In bibliographies and other references, a colon is used between a title and subtitle—even when no punctuation appears on the original title page, since publishers commonly drop the colons before subtitles on such pages. But when a dash is used in the title instead of a colon, the dash should be retained in any reference to that work.

5. In bibliographies and notes, a colon is used to separate a volume number from an issue or page number.

Karen Burton Mains, "Healing the Wounds of Long Ago," *Christian Herald* 110, no. 11 (December 1987): 22.

6. Place an unspaced colon between chapter and verse designations in Scripture references and between hours and minutes in time references.

John 3:16   7:21 A.M.

E. Dash

1. There are several kinds of dashes, varying in length and function. These can be indicated as follows:

Kind of dash	Typewritten	Typeset
hyphen	-	-
en dash	-	–
one-em dash	--	—
two-em dash	---	——
three-em dash	----	———

Apart from the hyphen, the em dash (—) is the most frequently used in ordinary manuscript writing. When used alone, the word *dash* usually refers to an em dash.

2. An em dash can be used to indicate the source of a quote when that quote is set off from the text, as in an epigraph or block quotation.

Alms are but the vehicles of prayer.—John Dryden
A man without religion is like a beast without a bridle.—Latin proverb

3. An em dash can indicate an abrupt shift in the continuity of a sentence or a thought or a strongly rhetorical turn of phrase.

Nothing in this world is to be taken seriously—nothing except the salvation of a soul.—Bishop Fulton Sheen
Feel for others—in your pocket.—C. H. Spurgeon

4. A dash may be used to insert parenthetical matter that carries special emphasis or importance to the main thrust of the sentence. (Parentheses should be used when the parenthetical matter is not as essential to the argument of the sentence.)

We must become so pure in heart—and it needs much practice—that we shall see God.—Henry Drummond
Mistress Anne Bradstreet—a woman and a Puritan no less—may be regarded as the first major American poet.

Erasmus Darwin (grandfather of Charles) and Lamarck postulated the inheritance of acquired characteristics.

5. When several items are listed and then summarized as a group by a single word in a concluding sentence or clause, a dash should separate the list from the concluding sentence or clause.

Wycliffe, Tyndale, Coverdale—all had a dream of seeing the Bible generally available in English. [*All* is the summarizing word in this case.]

6. Occasionally the dash may be used, like a colon, as a kind of pointer to direct the reader to something that follows an introductory phrase. It should be reserved, however, for those instances when a special emphasis is being placed on the words that follow the dash. In most cases a colon will suffice.

That is what we are here for—to do God's will.—Henry Drummond

7. In some circumstances the dash may be used in combination with other punctuation. When a dash immediately concludes a quotation and is immediately followed by the speaker reference, a comma should follow the dash. Often dashes are used in place of commas to introduce a parenthetical idea into a sentence; in these cases a question mark or exclamation point can be used in combination with the dash when appropriate.

"Mine is comic art—," Flannery O'Connor quipped.
Southwell knew the dangers—who more than he?—of returning to England.

8. In dialogue, broken, hesitating, or interrupted speech is indicated by an em dash. An en dash is used to indicate stuttering or the spelling out of words in dialogue.

"I can't—don't even ask—swear such an oath!"
"What was—" A peal of thunder interrupted him.
"I s–see. B–but why?" asked Brother Juniper.
"I can't remember; is Niebuhr spelled N–I–E or N–E–I?"

9. An en dash is used to indicate successive, inclusive, or continuing numbers, as in dates, page numbers, or Scripture references. (See pages 101–2 for special rules governing elision of numbers.)

    1852–53   May–June 1967   pp. 29–41   John 4:3–6:2

10. An en dash should replace a hyphen in a compound adjective if one of the adjectives is already hyphenated or is made up of two words.

    the Norman–Anglo-Saxon church   pre–Civil War
    an Old Testament–New Testament contrast

11. A two-em dash indicates that letters have been omitted from a word.

    A dilapidated sign caused the confusion; it read, "Bay View Church; R——ent [Repent] Now!"
    The book was signed C. W——s [Williams?].

12. A three-em dash indicates that an entire word has been omitted.

    A certain pastor in the village of —— was known to have cooperated with the Nazis.

F. Parentheses

1. Parentheses may be used to expand, comment upon, explain, or define a point, or may be used to make an aside, whether or not it is closely related to the first part of the sentence. While commas and dashes can also be used to set off parenthetical statements, commas are best used when an extremely close affinity exists between the inserted element and the rest of the sentence. Dashes that enclose a parenthetical idea, on the other hand, convey more of a sense of energy, urgency, interruption, or immediacy.

    William of Ockham (remembered in the phrase "Ockham's Razor") left Avignon in 1328.

Lancelot Andrewes, who was said to have kept Christmas all the year, was noted for his hospitality.

For only love—which means humility—can cast out the fear which is the root of all war.—Thomas Merton

2. When lists are run into the text, parentheses are used around the numbers or letters.

The reasons are that (1) he was from Galilee, (2) he was the son of a carpenter . . . [do not use 1), 2)]

The historian was careful to distinguish between (1) Macarius Magnes, (2) Macarius of Alexandria, and (3) Macarius of Egypt.

3. Periods, question marks, and exclamation points should be placed outside a closing parenthesis when the parenthetical statement is inserted into a larger sentence, although a question mark or exclamation mark should be placed inside the closing parenthesis when it is part of the parenthetical statement itself.

Elizabeth Fry's activities reflected the many social concerns of her time (such as slavery, missions among the Indians, and the poor).

Dorothy Sayers published her first detective novel (could she have guessed how popular they would become?) just after establishing her teaching career.

4. Periods, question marks, and exclamation points should be placed inside the closing parenthesis when the entire sentence is enclosed in parentheses.

The Ephesus that Paul knew was the major trade center in the Roman province of Asia. (By A.D. 950 it had become a ghost town.)

5. When a parenthetical Scripture reference immediately follows a Scripture quotation, place any needed punctuation after the parenthetical reference. If the quotation itself requires a question mark or exclamation point, it should be placed with the text regardless of what punctuation follows the parenthesis.

"Jesus wept" (John 11:35), the shortest verse in Scripture, is often quoted out of context.

"Lord, are you going to wash my feet?" (John 13:6).

G. Brackets

1. Brackets are most commonly used to indicate an editorial comment, substitution, or explanation within quoted material. The bracketed word may either replace a word in the original or may be placed next to a word as an amplification.

   "The creed was first proposed by Eusebius [of Caesarea] in A.D. 325."

   "On September 2, 1666, [Richard Baxter] witnessed the Great Fire of London." or "On September 2, 1666, he [Richard Baxter] witnessed the Great Fire of London."

2. Brackets are also commonly used to mark a parenthetical statement made within an already parenthetical context ("parentheses within parentheses").

   Daniel interpreted the mysterious inscription ("Mene, mene, tekel, parsin" [Daniel 5:25]) immediately before Belshazzar's death.

H. Ellipses

1. The decision to use a four-dot or a three-dot ellipsis depends on the context. A three-dot ellipsis can indicate either (1) that words within a quoted sentence have been omitted or (2) that words at the beginning or end of a sentence have been omitted, leaving the sentence grammatically incomplete. A four-dot ellipsis (a period followed by a three-dot ellipsis) indicates an omission between two quoted sentences when that omission does not render those sentences grammatically incomplete. In other words, use a four-dot ellipsis when the context would ordinarily call for a period (that is, after a grammatically complete sentence).

"The more often he feels without acting . . . the less he will be able to feel," wrote Screwtape to Wormwood.

Job focuses on God, not on God's questions. He shows this by beginning his answer by saying, "I know that you . . ." (Job 42:2).

"Mother Teresa . . . is one such woman. . . . Malcolm Muggeridge has given her . . . the most beautiful tribute."—Kari Torjesen Malcolm

2. When an ellipsis falls at the end of a typeset line, only the four-dot ellipsis may be split over the line break, with the first dot (the period) remaining on the end of the first line and the three subsequent dots carrying over to the next line. A three-dot ellipsis may never be split.

Sheldon's preface began, "*In His Steps* was written in 1896. . . . The book has been translated into twenty-one languages."

3. When a question mark or exclamation point precedes the omitted portion of the quotation, then that punctuation mark is used in place of the period and followed by a three-dot ellipsis.

"But now, Lord, what do I look for? . . . Do not make me the scorn of fools!" (Ps. 39:7–8).

4. Other punctuation, such as a comma, may be retained before or after the three-dot ellipsis if it helps clarify the meaning of the sentence or better shows what has been omitted.

"For he spoke, . . . he commanded, and it stood firm" (Ps. 33:9).

5. Use a three-dot ellipsis to indicate a trailing off of thought, daydreaming, or hesitation, although frequent use of ellipses for this purpose is discouraged. (But use a dash to indicate a sudden interpolation or an external interruption of thought or speech.)

If only the people would read the Bible . . . if only . . . , thought Frelinghuysen, *then God would bring about revival.*

Niebuhr—that is, Reinhold Niebuhr—was a pastor in Detroit in the twenties.

6. Unless the context demands it (usually with a sentence fragment), do not place ellipsis points before or after a verse or a portion of a Scripture verse. An introductory word such as *and, for, but, verily,* or *therefore* may be omitted from the beginning of a Scripture verse without inserting ellipsis points.

> "God so loved the world that he gave his one and only Son" (John 3:16). [The word *For* has been omitted.]

I. Quotation Marks

1. Quotation marks are most commonly used to set off material quoted from a written source or to indicate dialogue. These uses, called *direct discourse,* should be distinguished from *indirect discourse,* which should not be set off by quotation marks.

> "Few individuals have done as much as St. Francis to show Christians the way of peace," wrote Morton Kelsey. [written source]
> The pastor responded, "In witnessing, remember that we are only beggars advising other beggars where to find food." [dialogue]
> Chesterton referred to coincidences as spiritual puns. [indirect discourse]

2. Double quotation marks are used for most purposes. Single quotation marks are used almost exclusively to indicate quotes within quotes. If a further level of interior quotation is needed, double quotation marks are reverted to.

> "But the angel said to them, 'Do not be afraid'" (Luke 2:10).
> John read Job 42:1–4 aloud, "Then Job replied to the Lord, 'I know that you can do all things; . . . You said, "Listen now, and I will speak"'" (Job 42:1–2, 4).

3. Quotation marks are occasionally used when a word or phrase is meant to be ironic. Since a reader can easily

misunderstand the writer's intention, the careful writer should be able to convey irony without this device. Slang words and jargon should only be placed in quotation marks when they are not part of the speaker's normal vocabulary. Quotation marks are best used with slang words or colloquial expressions when a strong emphasis is desired; even then they should be used with discernment and restraint.

> He resented the church's demand for a "free-will" offering.
> She could not be sure to what extent he had been "born again."

4. When other punctuation marks are used with quotation marks, correct placement depends on the context. In direct discourse, for instance, periods and commas usually go inside a closing quote mark; question marks and exclamation points usually go inside closing quotes, although they may go outside if the sentence structure calls for it. As a general rule, colons and semicolons are placed outside.

> As he read the creed he hesitated before saying, ". . . the quick and the dead"; a more modern translation would read, ". . . the living and the dead."
> " 'Why were you searching for me?' he asked. 'Didn't you know I had to be in my Father's house?' " (Luke 2:49).
> Why was the 1560 Geneva Bible called the "Breeches Bible"?

5. Block quotations do not normally begin or end with quotation marks. Note, however, that block quotations should retain any and all quotation marks that appear in the original. Also, epigraphs (whether on a separate page or at the beginning of a chapter) and other quotations used for display should not be enclosed in quotation marks. Only those quotation marks that appear in the original should be retained in epigraphs.

6. In the case of run-in quotations, use single quotation marks for quotes within the quote. (See rule 2 in this section.) But when only the interior quotation is excerpted,

the single quotation marks are dropped as long as the context is clear.

Revelation 22:20 reads, "He who testifies to these things says, 'Yes, I am coming soon.' " [quote within the quote]
Remember what the Spirit of Christ said to John in Revelation 22:20: "Yes, I am coming soon." [no single quotes used]

7. Except in direct discourse, the words *yes* and *no* do not need to be enclosed in quotation marks.

   Although saying yes to Jesus doesn't solve all of life's problems, saying no can be a bigger problem in itself.

8. The titles of short poems, essays, articles in periodicals, short stories, chapters in books, individual television shows (series are set in italics), radio programs, paintings and other individual works of art, hymns, songs, and other short musical compositions are set in quotation marks. (Compare these titles with those that require italics on pages 72–73). Nicknames of people require quotation marks when used with the full name.

   He referred to the "Speaking Out" column in last month's *Christianity Today.*
   PBS broadcast Muggeridge's television show "God's Spies" from his series, *The Third Testament.*
   They worked on the repair of Michelangelo's "Pietá."
   William Ashley ("Billy") Sunday, *but* Billy Sunday

9. When a chapter begins with a quotation, an opening quotation mark is not used if the sentence begins with an oversized initial capital, though the closing quotation mark should be retained.

J. Solidus (Slash)

1. An unspaced solidus or an en dash may be used to indicate that a season or other period of time spans two consecutive years, although the en dash is preferred.

   winter 1620/21   fiscal year 1987–88

2. If two or more lines of poetry are run into the text, a solidus (with a word space on both sides) is used to indicate line breaks.

> Many people who quote, "God moves in a mysterious way, / His wonders to perform," (from the hymn by William Cowper) mistakenly believe they are quoting the Bible.

K. Apostrophe

1. An 's should be used to form the plurals of abbreviations with periods, lowercase letters used as nouns, and capital letters that would be confusing if only s were added.

> M.D.'s and Th.D.'s   x's and y's   S's, A's, I's but Ts, Ds

2. If years are abbreviated to two numerals, they should be preceded by an apostrophe. No apostrophe, however, should go before the s in decade designations in numerals. (In most cases the form *sixties*, *seventies*, etc. is preferred to the form '60s, '70s, etc.)

> They graduated with the class of '82.
> It should not have surprised us when the seminarians of the '60s became the ministers of the '70s. [Preferred version: ". . . when the seminarians of the sixties became the ministers of the seventies."]

3. An apostrophe is used to denote possession (see rules for possessives on pages 75–77.)

> the prophet's writings   the apostles' ministry
> the women's advice   George MacDonald's books

4. An apostrophe is also used in a contraction to indicate the absence of a letter or letters. Contractions should be reserved for dialogue and informal writing in which it is important to preserve a speaker's or author's colloquial tone. Contractions, of course, are always preserved in direct quotation. Otherwise contractions should be used sparingly in formal writing.

"Here's to us all—God bless us every one," said Tiny Tim.
I'm not tempted by despair; where there's life, there's hope.
[informal, colloquial]
I am reminded of Sir Thomas More's idea that there is no sorrow on
earth that heaven cannot heal. [formal; "I am" and "there is"
are not contracted]

L. Accent Marks

1. Accent marks are most commonly used with certain
   foreign words. The following is a list of the most common
   accents:

acute accent	é	hacek	ĕ
breve	ŏ	macron	ō
cedilla	ç	tilde	ñ
circumflex	ê	umlaut	ö
grave accent	è		

2. For foreign words that have become common in English,
   no simple rules can be given for when to retain an accent
   and when to drop it. When a specific word is in question,
   this manual recommends conforming to the first entry of
   that word in *Webster's Ninth New Collegiate Dictionary*,
   which tends to retain accents where many other style
   manuals and dictionaries drop them. When in doubt, it is
   best to retain the accent.

3. Accents are also used in poetry to indicate unexpected
   syllabification for purposes of scansion. The accent in
   these cases should always be retained in direct quotes.

   > For, though I knew His love Who followèd,
   > Yet was I sore adread
   > Lest, having Him, I must have naught beside.
   > —Francis Thompson, "Hound of Heaven"

M. Miscellaneous Rules

1. When more than one type style is used in a sentence,
   periods and commas are set in the same font as the word
   that immediately precedes them. The brackets around the

word *sic* should not be set in italics. Colons, semicolons, question marks, exclamation points, quotation marks, and parentheses should be in the font that is called for by the context of the sentence.

Newman followed the *Apologia,* written in 1864, with *Grammar of Assent.*
(see paragraph 6a)   [*sic*]
"The prayer ended with a *Deo gratias.*" [The closing quotes are in roman type.]

2. When an abbreviation ends a sentence, the abbreviating period will also serve as the period to the sentence. All other punctuation, however, is used in combination with an abbreviating period.

After receiving his M.Div., he did not go on for his Th.D.
Who first compiled the B.C.P.?

3. When two different punctuation marks are needed in the same place in a sentence, only the more emphatic mark is used.

In which poem does Hopkins write, "O world wide of its good!" [No final question mark is added.]
"What shall we do with Jesus?" Moody asked the congregation. [No comma is used after the question mark.]
Does he really believe you can serve both God and mammon! [No question mark is used.]

4. In references or in running text, when a title of a work ends in a question mark or an exclamation point, any period or comma that would ordinarily follow that title is dropped. In running text, when dropping a comma might result in ambiguity, however, the question mark or exclamation point in the title should be dropped in favor of the comma. Colons and semicolons, however, can be used in combination with question marks or exclamation points in titles and should be retained.

Morrison, Frank. *Who Moved the Stone?* London: Faber and Faber, 1930. [no period after the title]

After reading Philip Yancey's *Where Is God When It Hurts,* I began looking for his other books. [question mark dropped in favor of comma to avoid misreading]

He had read Francis Schaeffer's *How Then Shall We Live?*; it made a deep impression on him.

5. On those rare occasions when ditto marks are needed, a double prime mark (″) is used in typeset copy. Ordinary quotation marks are used in typewritten copy.

III.
CAPITALIZATION

A. General Rules

1. The purpose of capitalization is to show that a specific thing is being referred to, not a general thing. In publications in the United States the tendency is to avoid capitalization wherever it is not needed for this purpose. Many words formerly capitalized may now be lowercased without loss of clarity. While this chapter defines specific rules of capitalization, it also reflects the general trend toward using the lowercase.

2. Authors occasionally choose to capitalize certain terms that are part of a special vocabulary. Authors should inform the editor of these special usages and should in all cases establish a consistent pattern of capitalization.

3. In titles, lowercase the articles *a*, *an*, and *the*, except when the article is the first word of the title. Also lowercase all prepositions of four or fewer letters.

4. The first word of a hyphenated compound in a title or heading is always capitalized. If the compound is ordinarily hyphenated, the second word should not be capped. But capitalize the second word if it is a temporary compound or a coordinate term. Also capitalize the first word following a colon or a dash in a title.

Orange-Red Leaves   *Old-fashioned Gospel Hymns*
"Ninety-five Theses"   *High-School Ministry*
King-sized Mistakes   *Paul: A Life*

5. An adverb in a title should always be capitalized, even though the same word might not be capped when used as a preposition.

Looking Up to Jesus   *Steady As She Goes*
Coming In Out of the Rain   *A Walk in the Rain*

6. Capitalize the first word of an internal sentence, and usually capitalize the first word after a question mark.

She wondered, *Why haven't they called yet?*
When did you see him? And where?

7. Capitalize the first word after a colon if it introduces a complete passage or sentence having independent meaning, announces a definition, or introduces a formal description.

William Carey will be remembered for this phrase: Expect great things from God; attempt great things for God.
Merton's conflict was this: Would the Trappists even accept him, or would the army draft him first?

8. As racial designations the terms *black* and *white* are lowercased both as adjectives and nouns unless part of a phrase that would require capitalization.

Many blacks and whites marched together in the sixties.
a black gospel choir   the Black Muslims

B. Proper Nouns and Personal Names

1. Consult a dictionary or a biographical reference book if in doubt about foreign names that use particles. Several guidelines have merit. Particles in English and North American names are usually capped unless a family prefers a lowercase form. French, Italian, Portuguese, Spanish, Dutch, and German particles are usually lowercased if a name or title precedes them. In French names

Le, L', La, and *Les* are usually capped, but *de* and *d'* are not capitalized. For some names, the particle is commonly dropped when the last name is used alone; when a particle is not preceded by a first name or a title (except for French names using *de* or *d'*), capitalize it. A particle is always capitalized at the beginning of a sentence.

Ludwig van Beethoven
  but Beethoven
Werner Von Braun
Catherine de Médici
Thomas De Quincey

Charles de Gaulle
Corrie ten Boom
Leonardo da Vinci
  but Da Vinci
Henry Van Dyke

2. Generally the formal names of governmental organizations and bodies are capitalized. As adjectives they are lowercased.

United States Congress; Congress; congressional
House of Representatives; the House; the lower house of Congress
Committee on Foreign Affairs; Foreign Affairs Committee; the committee
Parliament; parliamentary; early parliament; Houses of Parliament
General Assembly of Illinois; Illinois legislature; assembly

3. Generic terms and informal terms for governmental bodies are lowercased.

administration
cabinet
the crown
district
electoral college
federal government

government
ministry
office
precinct
state
state's attorney

4. When a title follows a person's name or when it is used in place of the person's name, it is lowercased.

President Kennedy; John F. Kennedy, president of the United States; the president of the United States; the president
Gen. George S. Patton; General Patton; the general
Elizabeth II, queen of England; Queen Elizabeth; the queen

5. Names of political organizations are capitalized. But words such as *party* and *movement* are not.

Common Market	Fascist party
Communist party	Fascists
Communists	Holy Alliance
Democratic platform	Republican convention

6. To indicate broad systems of economic, philosophic, or political thought, the noun or adjective should be lowercased. If the word is derived from a proper name, however, it should be capitalized.

bolshevism	democracy	Marxism-Leninism
communism	liberalism	Nazism
conservatism	Malthusianism	socialism

7. Most period designations are lowercased (except for those derived from proper nouns and those that have come to be capitalized by tradition).

Age of Reason	first century
age of steam	Middle Ages
ancient Greece	Paleolithic times
Christian Era	space age
colonial period	Stone Age
Eighteenth Dynasty	the twenties
Era of Good Feeling	*but* the Roaring Twenties
fin de siècle	Victorian era

8. Most names for specific historical events are capitalized. Popular names and nicknames for most cultural or historical moments or events are capitalized.

California Gold Rush	Industrial Revolution
Cold War	Kentucky Derby
Depression	Pickett's Charge
Fall of Rome	Prohibition
Great Depression	Reconstruction
Holocaust	World War I

9. Most nouns and adjectives referring to general artistic, academic, religious, or philosophic schools of thought are

lowercased. When they are derived from proper nouns, however, they are capitalized. Discretion is required, and in any given work, a particular term must be treated consistently.

Aristotelian	cubism	neoclassicism
baroque	Gregorian chant	impressionism
Cartesian	classical	romanticism
naturalism	Platonism	transcendentalism

10. The rules for the capitalization of geographical nouns and adjectives are many and varied. Most specific questions can be answered by referring to a reference work. The following brief summary and the list that follows it should help with most standard names.

Capitalize *Western, Eastern,* etc., when they are part of a formal place name or are used in the sense of political division. *Continent* and *Continental* are capitalized to designate Europe. Such terms as *mountain* and *lake* are capitalized when they are part of a formal place name.

the East; Far East(ern); Orient(al); the Near East
the Western world *but* the western plains
the Continent (Europe) *but* the Australian continent
the North Atlantic *but* northern Atlantic
Southerner (Civil War) *but* southerner (common usage)
a Westerner (from the Western Hemisphere) *but* a westerner (from
    the western United States)
the East Coast or the West Coast
the Arctic Circle *but* the equator
the Tropic of Cancer *but* the tropics
Ohio River *but* the Ohio and Wabash rivers; the river Nile
Lake Michigan; Lakes Huron and Michigan

11. As a general rule capitalize adjectives derived from place names or personal names.

Brussels sprouts	Wycliffite pamphlet
French bread	Shakespearean drama

12. A term indicating a family relationship is lowercased when it is used generically or when it is preceded by a

modifier. It should be capitalized when it is used as a family member's common appellation, that is, when it is used as if it were a proper name.

"Will Cousin Ed lead the singing, Dad?" his son asked hopefully. "No, Son, but Mother's brothers and her sister Carol will sing solos."

13. Affectionate terms, such as *honey, dear, sweetheart*, and so on, are lowercased.

C. Biblical and Religious Terms

Few matters of style have caused as much consternation to writers and editors of religious books as the capitalization of biblical and religious terms. Since Victorian times there has been a tendency to overcapitalize, a style that looks religiose and antiquated to most modern readers. Still, the character of religious publishing requires that general rules be established.

1. Capitalization of pronouns referring to persons of the Trinity has been a matter of debate. Although both styles are acceptable and common, this manual encourages the use of lowercase pronouns. Many religious publishers and most general publishers have adopted this style, in part, to conform to the styles of the most commonly used Bible versions (the King James Version and the *New International Version*). Obviously there are many situations in which the capitalization of such pronouns may be preferred, for instance, in books of a highly devotional nature or when the author quotes extensively from a Bible version that uses the capitalized style (such as the *New American Standard Bible*), or when antecedents might become easily confused in closely written text. Even in the last case a careful writer should be able to make the meaning clear without capitalization. Before the editing process begins, the author should discuss his or her preference with the editor. When pronouns for

deity are capitalized, though, the words *who* and *whom* should not be.

2. Capitalize all names for the persons of the Trinity. Also capitalize names of deities from other faiths and from mythology.

Adonai	Holy Spirit	Messiah
Allah	Isis	Paraclete
Christ	Jehovah	Ra
El	Jesus	Shiva
God	Jupiter	Yahweh

3. Common epithets for persons of the Trinity, biblical characters, or figures in church history should be capitalized.

Alpha and Omega	Man of Sorrows
Ancient of Days	Son of Man
Comforter	St. John the Divine
Divine Doctor	Venerable Bede
King of Kings	Virgin Mary

4. Judgment must be exercised in determining which words and phrases are epithets and therefore capitalized, and which are merely descriptive and lowercased.

the Twelve *but* the twelve disciples
the Almighty *but* almighty God
the Good Shepherd *but* the second person of the Trinity

5. The words *apostle* and *prophet* are lowercased unless used as part of a common epithet that has come to have the force of a proper name.

the apostle John *but* the Beloved Apostle
the apostle Paul *but* the Apostle to the Gentiles
the prophet Jeremiah *but* the Weeping Prophet

6. The word *pharaoh* should be capitalized only when it is used as a proper name, which is, in most cases, when it is used without an article. When an article precedes it, it is lowercased as a common noun.

Moses was raised in Pharaoh's household.
At first he was afraid to address the pharaoh.

7. Official religious titles of modern or historical personages are capitalized according to the same rules as secular titles (see page 47). When an official title precedes a person's name, it is capitalized. When it follows or when it is used in place of the person's name, it is lowercased. General names for religious offices are also lowercased. Also, purely descriptive titles should be lowercased.

Archbishop Robert Runcie *but* the archbishop of Canterbury; the archbishop
Father Patrick O'Neil *but* the father
Bishop John Fisher *but* John Fisher, bishop of Rochester
Pope John Paul II *but* the pope
the ministry, the papacy, the bishopric, the pastorate
evangelist Billy Graham

8. Names and common epithets for Satan are capitalized.

Beast	the Devil	Evil One
Beelzebub	Dragon	Father of Lies

9. Most adjectives derived from proper names are capitalized. Adjectives and adverbs derived from the words *God* and *Satan*, however, are usually lowercased.

Aaronic priesthood	Isaian passages
Augustinian arguments	Matthean version
godlike power	Pauline writings
godly woman	satanic rites

10. All names and common epithets for the Bible and for the sacred writings of other traditions are capitalized. Note, however, that the word *bible* is lowercased when used in a figurative sense.

Good Book	Scripture	Vedas
Koran	Talmud	the Word

The Oxford English Dictionary is the bible of English-language studies.

11. Adjectives and adverbs derived from names for the Bible or other sacred writings are lowercased, although the term *Vedic* is commonly capitalized.

apocryphal   scriptural
biblically   talmudic

12. Names and nicknames of well-known or important historical versions and editions of Scripture are capitalized and set in roman type.

King James Version   Vinegar Bible
Syriac Version   Vulgate

13. Names for all books of the Bible, the Apocrypha, and pseudobiblical writings are capitalized. The words *book*, *gospel*, *letter*, *psalm*, and *epistle* are generic terms that specify different forms of written documents. They are lowercased unless they form part of the actual title of a book as given in the specific translation of the Bible being used.

Job, the book of Job [NIV], *but* the Book of Job [MLB]
John, John's gospel, the gospel of John [NIV], *but* the Gospel According to John [KJV], the Gospel of John [PHILLIPS]
Corinthians 1, First Corinthians, Paul's first epistle to the Corinthians, the first book of Corinthians, *but* the First Letter of Paul to the Corinthians [RSV]
the Gospel of Thomas [actual title]
the Protevangelion
Psalm 139
the Twenty-third Psalm *but* a psalm of David

14. Generally the word *gospel* is lowercased when used in a general sense or to indicate a style of preaching or sacred music. It may be capitalized when the specific New Testament concept of the Good News of God's redemption in the person of Christ is intended, and capitalization may be preferred in formal theological writing.

gospel music   the Gospel of Christ
gospel revival   the true Gospel
gospel tent   the Gospel of salvation

15. Names for specific parts, groupings, or passages of the Bible are capitalized when those names have come to be used as equivalents of titles.

Accession Psalms	Minor Prophets
General Epistles	New Testament
Gospels	Pentateuch
Historical Books	Poetical Books
Lord's Prayer	Synoptic Gospels
Love Chapter	Wisdom Literature

16. Judgment must be exercised in determining when names for specific parts, groupings, or passages of Scripture are merely descriptive and when they have come to have the force of actual titles. When in doubt, lowercase.

the Ten Commandments *but* the first commandment
the Gospel According to Matthew [RSV] *but* Matthew's gospel
the Gospels *but* the four gospels
the Epistle of Paul to the Romans [MLB] *but* Paul's Roman epistle
the Psalms *but* David's psalms [to distinguish those that David wrote]
the Book of Jeremiah [RSV] *but* Jeremiah's book of prophecies

17. The word *law* is capitalized when it refers to the Pentateuch as a whole or to the Ten Commandments.

Mosaic Law *but* Davidic law
the Law [Pentateuch] *but* the law [as opposed to grace]
the Law of Moses *but* a law of Moses

18. The word *parable*, like the words *book, gospel, letter, psalm,* and *epistle,* is lowercased as a descriptive term, as are any descriptive words that accompany it. Words describing specific parables should only be capitalized when they are proper nouns. In works that focus heavily and repeatedly on specific parables, the word *parable* and its accompanying words may be capitalized as formal titles.

the parable of the prodigal son
the parable of the good Samaritan
the parable of the wicked serving men *but*
the Parable of the Wicked Serving Men [if that form is used
  repeatedly as the equivalent of a title]

19. Accepted names for major biblical events, such as events
in the life of Christ, are set in lowercase when they have a
general reference and use. Such events are capitalized,
however, when used without modification, attribution, or
identification. In a passage in which there are multiple
references to the same event, it is acceptable to make
capitalization uniform even when some references are
modified and some are not, and when there is no
ambiguity of meaning.

the nativity of Christ *but* the Nativity
the crucifixion of Jesus *but* the Crucifixion
the captivity of the Jews *but* the Captivity
the creation of the universe *but* the Creation [the act, not the things
  created]
How long were the six days of Creation? *but* God looked over all
  his creation and said, "Very good!"

20. Names for important biblical objects are generally lowercased unless they are used to convey a specific and
commonly understood theological significance.

Noah's ark   the seven seals   the brazen altar   the tent
the cross [the wooden object] *but* the Cross [the event]

21. Many specific names of sacred concepts and objects of
veneration, especially those associated with the persons of
the Trinity, were once capitalized. The modern practice
is to lowercase them. Care must be taken to distinguish
between those words that are common nouns and
therefore lowercased, and those that form parts of
epithets for people, which should be capitalized. Note
that the names for a few legendary sacred objects have
become so common in literature that they are traditionally capitalized: the True Cross, the Holy Grail.

the blood of Christ, the holy name of Jesus
the light of Christ in the world *but* the Light of the World

22. Most names for biblical eras are lowercased. Care must be exercised in determining whether the name refers to an era and therefore lowercased, or to a specific event and therefore capitalized.

the age of the prophets
the last days *but* the Last Day
the millennial kingdom *but* the Millennium
the exilic period *but* the Exile

23. The titles of creeds, confessions, and other important documents of church history are capitalized and set in roman type.

Apostles' Creed   Thirty-nine Articles
Heidelberg Catechism   Westminster Confession

24. Common names for religious seasons, holy days, feast days, saints' days, and religious festivals and observances are capitalized.

Advent	Communion	Holy Week
Ash Wednesday	Conversion of	Michaelmas
Baptism	Saint Paul	Passover
Christian Unity	Epiphany	Saint Valentine's
Week	Holy Communion	Day

25. Names of specific sacraments and rites are commonly lowercased, except those indicating the Communion or the Eucharist, which are traditionally capitalized. The seven sacraments recognized by the Roman Catholic Church are baptism, confirmation, the Eucharist, penance, anointing of the sick (preferred to the term *extreme unction*), holy orders, and matrimony. Names for general systems of religious rites (such as Latin Rite, Roman Rite, Eastern Rites, and Western Rites) are capitalized.

Holy Eucharist	Lord's Table	Sacred Host
last rites	Masonic Rites	sacred rites

26. Names of official denominations and the common adjectives derived from them are capitalized according to denominational usage.

Baptist	Church of God	Roman Catholic
Brethren	Episcopal	Seventh-day
Christian Reformed	Methodism	Adventism

27. The word *church* is lowercased unless it forms part of a formal or official name of a specific denomination. For instance, since there is no official denomination called "the Reformed church," *church* is lowercased. In "the Christian Reformed Church," however, it is capped as part of the official name of the denomination. *Church* is also lowercased when used in a general sense or to refer to the universal church of all believers.

Baptist church	Methodist church
Christ's church	Protestant church
the church	Reformed church
church and state	Reformed Church in America
Episcopal Church	Roman Catholic Church
invisible church	United Methodist Church

28. Words such as *church, chapel, temple, meeting, synagogue, tabernacle, mission, ministry, hall, fellowship, cathedral, congregation,* and *assembly* are capitalized when they form part of the official name of a local religious meeting place. Otherwise, as common nouns they are lowercased.

the Chapel Hill Bible Church *but* the church
Brick Bible Chapel *but* the chapel
the Temple Emmanuel *but* the temple
St. Paul's Cathedral *but* the cathedral
Westminster Presbyterian Church *but* the local Presbyterian church

29. The names for major historical religious groups and movements, and the adjectives derived from them, are generally capitalized.

Pharisee	Puritan(ism)
Protestant(ism)	Pentecostal(ism)

30. The names of broad modern religious movements that are not official denominations and the names of general religious philosophies, and the adjectives derived from all such words, should be lowercased. By the same principle, the terms *liberal* and *conservative* usually have a generic or relative use and should be lowercased.

agnostic(ism)	evangelical(ism)
charismatic renewal	new agism
charismatics	secular humanism
conservative church	theologians
ecumenical, ecumenism	theistic

31. The word *movement* is capitalized only if the adjective that precedes it is capitalized. Tradition may be a factor in whether or not to capitalize; recognized historical movements are more likely to be capitalized, while contemporary movements are not.

    the Pentecostal Movement *but* the charismatic movement
    the Holiness Movement *but* the ecumenical movement

32. Common names for major periods and events in church history are generally capitalized unless they are purely descriptive.

    Great Awakening *but* the age of revivalism
    Middle Ages *but* the medieval era
    Reformation

33. Place names in Scripture are ordinarily capitalized, but terms like *heaven, hell, gehenna, sheol,* and *hades* are generally lowercased as common nouns. The word *paradise* is capitalized only when it refers to the Garden of Eden. The word *kingdom* is lowercased except when it forms part of a geographical place name.

    Abyss *but* hades, sheol
    Garden of Eden
    kingdom of God, Christ's kingdom, *but* the Upper Kingdom
    New Jerusalem *but* heaven, paradise, the abode of the saints

34. Common epithets for places are capitalized. Care must be exercised to distinguish between those words and phrases that are epithets and therefore capitalized, and those that are merely descriptive and lowercased.

the City of David *but* the city where David reigned
the Eternal City
the Holy Land *but* the land of Jesus
the Land of Promise *but* the land of Canaan

35. Capitalization of commonly used religious terms:

Aaronic priesthood
Abba
Abrahamic covenant
Abraham's bosom
Abraham's side
Abyss, the
Adonai
Advent, the
Advent season
Advocate, the
age of grace
age to come, the
agnosticism
Almighty, the
almighty God
Alpha and Omega (Christ)
amillenarian
amillennial(ism)(ist)
ancient Near East
Ancient of Days, the (God)
angel (cap if theophany)
angel Gabriel, the
angel of the Lord (cap if
    theophany)
Annunciation, the
Anointed, the (Christ)
Anointed One, the (Christ)
anointing of the sick

ante-Christian
ante-Nicene fathers
anti-Catholic
antichrist (the general spirit)
Antichrist (the person)
anti-Christian
antichurch
antilegomena
anti-God
anti-Semitism
anti-Trinitarian
Apocalypse, the (Revelation
    of John)
apocalyptic
Apocrypha, the
apocryphal (cap only if
    Apocrypha is meant)
apostle Peter, et al.
Apostle to the Gentiles (Paul)
apostles, the
Apostles' Creed
apostolic age
apostolic benediction (2 Cor. 13)
apostolic council (Acts 15)
apostolic faith
archangel
ark, the (Noah's)
ark of testimony

ark of the covenant
Arminian(ism)
Ascension, the
Ascension Day
Athanasian Creed
atheism, -ist
Atonement, the
Augsburg Confession

babe in the manger, the
baby Jesus, the
Babylonian captivity (Jews)
baptism
Baptism, the (of Christ)
Battle of Armageddon (final
    battle)
Beast, the (Antichrist)
Beatitudes, the
Beelzebub
Being (God)
Beloved Apostle, the
Betrayal, the
Bible, the
Bible Belt, the
Bible school
biblical
blessed name (Christ)
Blessed Virgin
blood of Christ
body of Christ (the church)
Book, the (Bible)
book of Genesis, et al.
Book of Life (book of judgment)
Book of the Covenant
Book of the Law
Book of the Twelve, the
Book of Truth
boy Jesus, the
brazen altar
Bread of Life (Bible or Christ)
Bridegroom, the (Christ)

bride of Christ (the church)
brotherhood of man
burnt offering

Calvary
Calvinist(ic), -ism
Canon, the (Scripture)
canon of Scripture, the
Captivity, the (of the Jews)
catechumen
catholic (universal)
Catholic Church (Roman
    Catholic)
Catholic Epistles (James, et al.)
Catholicism
Celestial City (abode of the
    redeemed)
charismatic
charismatic church
charismatic movement
cherub(im)
chief priest
Chief Shepherd (Christ)
child Jesus
children of Israel
chosen people (Jews)
Christ
Christ child
christen(ing)
Christian (n. and adj.)
Christian era
Christianize, -ization
Christianlike
Christlike
Christmas Day
Christmas Eve
Christmastide
Christocentrism
Christology, -ical
church, the (body of Christ)
church (building)

church (service)
church age
church and state
church fathers (the Fathers)
church in America
church invisible
church militant
Church of England
Church of Rome
church triumphant
church universal
church visible
City of David (Jerusalem,
    Bethlehem)
Comforter, the (Holy Spirit)
commandment (first, et al.)
Commandments, the Ten
Communion (sacrament)
confirmation
Counselor, the
covenant, the
covenant of grace
covenant of works
Creation, the (the act)
creation, the (the result)
Creator, the
Cross, the (the event)
cross (the wooden object)
crown
Crucifixion, the
crucifixion of Christ
Crusades, the
Curse, the

Daniel's Seventieth Week
Davidic covenant
Davidic law
Day of Atonement (Yom Kippur)
day of grace
Day of Judgment
Day of Pentecost

Day of the Lord
Dead Sea Scrolls
Decalogue
Defender (God)
deism, -ist
Deity, the
deity of Christ
Deluge, the (the Flood)
demon(ic)
Deuteronomic
devil, a
Devil, the (Satan)
Diaspora
disciples
dispensation(alism)(alist)
dispensation of the Law
Dispersion, the
divided kingdom (period of
    history)
divine
Divine Father
divine guidance
Divine Providence (God)
Divinity, the (God)
divinity of Christ, the
Door, the (Christ)
doxology
Dragon, the (Satan)

early church
Easter Sunday
Eastern church
Eastern religions
Eastern Rites
ecumenism, -ical
El
Eleven, the
Elohim
El Shaddai
Emmaus road
end times, the

Enemy, the (Satan)
Epiphany
epistle (John's epistle, et al.)
epistle to the Romans
Epistles, the (NT apostolic letters)
eschatology, -ical
Eternal, the (God)
Eternal City (Rome)
eternal God, the
eternal life
eternity
Eucharist
Evangel (any of the four gospels)
evangelical (adj.)
evangelicals, -ism
Evangelist (gospel writer)
evangelist (someone who
    evangelizes)
Evil One, the (Satan)
Exile, the
Exodus, the (from Egypt)
extrabiblical
extreme unction

faith, the (Christianity)
faith-healing
Fall, the
fall of man
false christs
False Prophet (of Revelation)
false prophet(s)
Father (God)
Father of Lies (Satan)
fatherhood of God
Fathers, the (of the church)
Feast (meaning Passover)
Feast of Booths (Sukkoth)
Feast of Esther (Purim)
Feast of Firstfruits
Feast of Tabernacles

Feast of the Dedication
    (Hanukkah)
Feast of the Lights (Hanukkah)
Feast of the Passover (Pesach)
Feast of Unleavened Bread
First Adam
First Advent
First Cause, the
Firstborn, the (Christ)
first person of the Trinity
Flood, the
four gospels, the
fourth gospel, the
free will
fundamentalist(s), -ism
fundamentals of the faith

Galilean, the (Christ)
Garden of Eden
Garden of Gethsemane
gehenna
Gemara
General Epistles
Gentile, a (distinguished from
    Jew)
gentile laws
Gloria Patri
gnostic (generic)
Gnostic(ism) (specific sect)
God (Yahweh)
god (pagan)
Godhead (essential being of God)
godhead (godhood or godship)
godless
godlike
godly
God-man
godsend
God's house
Godspeed
God's Word (the Bible)

God's word (his promise)
godward
golden candlesticks, the
Golden Rule, the
Good Book, the
Good Friday
Good News, the
Good Samaritan
Good Shepherd (Jesus)
good shepherd, the parable
    of the
gospel (see pages 53–54)
gospel (John's gospel, et al.)
gospel of Matthew
Gospels, the
gospel truth
grain offering
Great Awakening, the
Great Commandment, the
Great Commission, the
Great High Priest, the
Great Judgment, the
Great Physician, the
Great Shepherd, the
Great Tribulation, the
Great White Throne, the
Ground of Being
Guide, the (Holy Spirit)

hades
Hagiographa
hagiographer
hagiographic
Hail Mary
Hallel
Hanukkah (Feast of the
    Dedication)
Head, the (Christ head
    of the church)
heaven (abode of the redeemed)
heavenly Father

Heidelberg Catechism
hell
Herodian
Herod's temple
high church
High Priest, the (Christ)
high priest, a
High Priestly Prayer, the
Historical Books, the
holiness
Holiness Movement, the
Holy Bible
Holy Book (Bible)
Holy City (present or New
    Jerusalem)
Holy Communion
holy day of obligation
Holy Eucharist
holy family
Holy Ghost (prefer Holy Spirit)
Holy Grail
Holy Land (Palestine)
Holy of Holies
holy oil
Holy One, the (God, Christ)
holy order(s)
Holy Place
Holy Roller
Holy Saturday
Holy Scriptures
Holy See
Holy Spirit
Holy Thursday
Holy Trinity
holy water
Holy Week (before Easter)
Holy Writ (Bible)
Holy Year (Catholic)
homologoumena
house of the Lord

Immaculate Conception, the
Immanuel
Incarnation, the
incarnation of Christ
infant Jesus, the
inner veil
Intercessor, the (Christ)
intertestamental
Isaian or Isaianic

Jacob's Trouble
Jehovah
Jeremian or Jeremianic
Jesus Prayer, the
Jewish Feast (Passover)
Jewish New Year (Rosh
    Hashanah)
Johannine
John the Baptist
John the Beloved
John the Evangelist
Jordan River (but the river
    Jordan)
Jubilee (year of emancipation)
Judaic
Judaica
Judaism, -ist, -istic
Judaize(r)
Judean
Judeo-Christian
judges, the
Judgment Day
judgment seat of Christ

kerygma
King (God or Jesus)
King James Version
kingdom, the
kingdom age
kingdom of God
kingdom of heaven

kingdom of Israel
kingdom of Satan
King of Glory (Christ)
King of Kings (Christ)
kingship of Christ
Kinsman-Redeemer
koinonia
Koran, koranic

Lady, our
lake of fire
Lamb, the (Christ)
Lamb of God
Lamb's Book of Life
land of Canaan
Land of Promise
Last Day, the
last days, the
Last Judgment, the
last rites
Last Supper, the
last times, the
Latin Rite
laver
law (as opposed to grace)
Law, the (Pentateuch)
Law of Moses, the
law of Moses, a (general)
Lawgiver (God)
Lent(en)
Levitical
Levitical decrees
liberal(ism)
Light (Truth or Christ)
Light of the World (Christ)
Litany, the (Anglican)
living God
living Word, the (Bible)
Logos, the
Lord, the
Lord of Hosts

Lord of Lords
Lord's Anointed, the (Christ)
Lord's Day, the
lordship of Christ
Lord's Prayer, the
Lord's Supper, the
Lord's Table, the
Lost Tribes
lost tribes of Israel
Love Chapter, the
low church
Lukan

Magi
Magnificat, the
Major Prophets, the (div. of OT)
major prophets (people)
Majority Text
mammon
Man, the (Jesus)
Man of Sin
Man of Sorrows
Marcan or Markan
Masorete
Masoretic text
Mass (liturgy of the Eucharist)
matrimony
Matthean
Mediator, the (Christ)
mercy seat
Messiah, the (Christ)
messiahship
messianic
midtribulation(al)
millenarian(ism)(ist)
millennial kingdom
Millennium, the
Minor Prophets, the (div. of OT)
minor prophets (people)
Miserere, the
Mishnah

modernist(s), -ism
moon-god
Mosaic
Mosaic Law (Pentateuch or Ten
    Commandments)
Most High, the
Mount of Olives
Mount of Transfiguration
Mount Olivet
Mount Olivet Discourse
Mount Sinai
Muhammad (preferred)
Muslim (preferred)

name of Christ, the
Nativity, the
nativity of Christ, the
Near East
Neo-Babylonian Empire
neo-orthodox(y)
neo-pentecostalism
Neoplatonic
new birth
New City (part of modern
    Jerusalem)
new covenant (NT)
new heaven and new earth
New Jerusalem (heaven)
New Testament church
Nicene Creed
Nicene fathers
Ninety-five Theses
non-Christian (n. and adj.)
Nonconformism, -ist
northern kingdom
Nunc Dimittis

Old City (part of modern
    Jerusalem)
old covenant (OT)
Olivet discourse

Omega, the
Omnipotent, the
One, the (but the one true God)
Only Begotten, the
only begotten of the Father
only begotten Son of God
orthodox(y)
outer court (of the Temple)

Palestinian covenant
Palm Sunday
papacy
parable of the prodigal son
Paraclete, the
paradise (heaven)
Paradise (Garden of Eden)
Parousia
partial Rapture
Paschal Lamb (Jesus)
Passion Sunday (fifth Sunday in
    Lent)
Passion Week
Passover
Passover Feast
Passover Lamb (Jesus)
Pastoral Epistles
Pastoral Letters
Patriarch, the (Abraham)
patriarch, a
Paul the apostle
Pauline Epistles
Paul's epistles
Paul's letters
peace offering
penance
Pentateuch
Pentecost
Pentecostal(ism)
person of Christ
(the three) persons of the Trinity
Pesach (Passover)

Petrine
Pharaoh (when used as name
    without article)
pharaoh, the (general)
pharisaic (attitude)
Pharisaic (in reference to
    Pharisees)
Pharisee
Pilgrims, the
pillar of cloud
pillar of fire
Poetic Books, the
pope, the
Pope John Paul II
postbiblical
post-Christian
postexilic
postmillennial(ism)(ist)
post-Nicene fathers
pre-Christian
predestination
premillenarian
premillennial(ism)(ist)
pretribulation(al)
priesthood of believers
priesthood of Christ
Prime Mover
Prince of Darkness
Prince of Peace (Christ)
Prison Epistles
Prison Letters
Prodigal Son, the
Promised Land (Canaan or
    heaven)
Promised One, the (Christ)
prophet Isaiah (etc.), the
Prophetic Books, the
prophets, the (people)
Prophets, the (books of OT)
Protestant(ism)
Providence (God)

providence of God
providential
Psalm 119 (etc.)
Psalms, the (OT book)
psalm, a
psalmic
psalmist, the
Psalter, the (the Psalms)
pseudepigrapha
pseudepigraphal
purgatory
Purim (Feast of Esther)

Qumran

rabbi
rabbinic(al)
Rapture, the
real presence
Received Text, the
Redeemer, the
Reformation
Reformed church
Reformed theology
Reformers
Resurrection, the
resurrection of Christ
rite(s)
Rock, the (Christ)
Roman Catholic Church
Roman Rite
Rosh Hashanah (Jewish New
    Year)

Sabbath (day)
sabbatical (n. and adj.)
sacrament(s)
sacramentalism, -ist
Sacramentarian(ism)
Sacred Host
sacred rite(s)

Sadducee
Sanhedrin
Satan
satanic
satanism
Savior
scribe
scriptural
Scripture(s) (Bible; n. and adj.)
scripture(s) (other religions)
Second Adam (Christ)
Second Advent, the
Second Coming, the
second coming of Christ
second person of the Trinity
seder
Semite, -ic, -ism
Septuagesima
Septuagint
seraph(im)
Sermon on the Mount
Serpent, the (Satan)
seven sacraments, the
Seventh-day Adventist
Seventieth Week
Shabuoth (Pentecost)
shalom
shalom aleichem
Shechinah
sheol
Shepherd Psalm, the
Shulammite
Sin-Bearer, the
sin offering
Solomon's temple
Son of God
Son of Man
sonship of Christ
southern kingdom
Sovereign Lord
stations of the cross

Sukkoth (Feast of Booths)
Sunday school
sun-god
Sun of Righteousness
Supreme Being, the
Sustainer (God)
synagogue
Synoptic Gospels
synoptics, the
synoptic writers, the

tabernacle, the (OT building)
table of shewbread
Talmud, talmudic
Tanach
Targum, targumic
Te Deum
temple, the (at Jerusalem)
Temptation, the
temptation in the desert, the
temptation of Christ, the
Ten Commandments (but the
    second commandment)
Ten Tribes, the
ten tribes of Israel, the
tent
Tent of Meeting
Tent of the Testimony
Testaments, the
Textus Receptus
third person of the Trinity
Thirty-nine Articles (Anglican)
throne of grace
Thummim
Time of Jacob's Trouble
Time of the Gentiles, the
time of the judges, the
tomb, the
Torah
Tower of Babel
Transfiguration, the

Transjordan
Tree of Knowledge of Good and
    Evil
Tree of Life
tribe of Judah
Tribulation, the (historical event)
Trinitarian
Trinity, the
Triumphal Entry
triune God
Twelve, the
twelve apostles, the
Twenty-third Psalm

unchristian
ungodly
united kingdom (of Israel)
universal church
universalism, -ist
unscriptural
Upanishads
Upper Room, the
Upper Room Discourse
Urim

vacation Bible school
Vedas, Vedic
viaticum
Victor, the (Christ)
Vine, the (Christ)
Virgin Birth, the
Virgin Mary, the
visible church
Vulgate

Water of Life (Christ)
Way, the (Christ)
Way, the Truth, and the Life
Western church
Western Rites
Westminster Catechism

Wicked One, the (Satan)
Wisdom Literature, the
wise men
Word, the (Bible or Christ)
Word made flesh (Christ)
Word of God (Bible)
Word of Life

Word of Truth, the
Writings, the

Yahweh
Year of Jubilee
Yom Kippur (Day of Atonement)
Yuletide

IV.
WORDS IN CONTEXT

A. Italics

1. Italics should be used with discretion. A careful writer should not need to use italics for emphasis, although a word or phrase may occasionally be italicized when a specific emphasis will not be clear to the reader any other way. Entire sentences or paragraphs should not be set in italics, since this will confuse the reader, nor should boldface be used in running text to achieve emphasis.

2. When the author expects certain foreign words or phrases to be unfamiliar to the reader, they should be set in italics. But foreign words and phrases that have become common in English should not be italicized. As a general rule, those foreign expressions that appear among the main entries of *Webster's Ninth New Collegiate Dictionary* do not require italics. Those not listed in the main entries of *Webster's* or else listed in the "Foreign Words and Phrases" section at the back of that dictionary are, in most cases, unfamiliar enough to require italics.

3. With the exception of *sic*, scholarly Latin words and abbreviations should be set in roman. Even words requiring italics when spelled out should be roman when abbreviated. Consult *Webster's* and CMS.

   ibid.   et al.   q.v.   i.e. (*id est*)

4. A person's thoughts and unspoken prayers, when expressed in the first person, may be set in italics, unlike spoken discourse, which is set in quotation marks.

> *I will lay my weapons upon the altar of Christ,* thought Ignatius as he rode toward Montserrat.
> *Dear Father,* prayed Augustine silently, *make me pure—but not quite yet!*

5. A word referred to as a word should be set in italics. Its definition may be set in roman type within quotation marks if it is a formal definition. But when a word is quoted from a specific context, quotation marks, not italics, should be used.

> Early Methodist ministers used the word *liberty* to describe an openness to God's Spirit in their preaching.
> By *feretory* hagiographers mean "a shrine in which a saint's bones are deposited and venerated." [formal definition]
> The word *world* has various meanings in Scripture; in John 3:16, for instance, the Evangelist writes "world" to denote the inhabitants of our planet, not the broader cosmos.

6. Technical terms or special terminology of any kind, especially when accompanied by a definition, are usually set in italics in the first reference and in roman type thereafter.

> Medieval theories of *impanation* asserted that the elements of Communion could be both the real presence of Christ and bread and wine at the same time. Impanation was condemned as heretical and is no longer propounded.

7. Italics are used for titles of certain works and for some names. (Compare the following list with the one given for quotation marks in rule 8 on page 39.) Italicize the titles of books; newspapers and magazines (except for the initial *the*); legal cases; formal groupings of paintings, sculpture, or other works of art; long poems or collections of poems; plays; feature-length films; operas, musicals, ballets, and

other long musical compositions; collections of shorter musical compositions; television series; record albums; and ships and aircraft (though the designations USS, SS, and HMS are not italicized). The word *magazine* is set lowercase and in roman type when it is not part of the official name of a publication: *Time* magazine; *Eternity* magazine; but *Parents' Magazine.*

A Severe Mercy (book)
the *Christian Science Monitor* (newspaper)
Christianity Today (magazine)
Roe v. Wade (court case)
Rodin's *Gates of Hell* (grouping of sculptures)
Milton's *Paradise Lost* (long poem)
Blake's *Songs of Innocence* (collection of poems)
Eliot's *The Cocktail Party* (play)
The Mission (film)
Amahl and the Night Visitors (opera)
The Nutcracker (ballet)
Jesus Christ Superstar (musical)
Bach's *Two-Part Inventions* (collection of musical compositions)
The Fugitive (television series)
John Michael Talbot's *Come to the Quiet* (recording)
USS *Constitution* (ship)
the shuttle *Challenger* (aircraft)

8. The initial article of a title may be dropped when syntax warrants it, such as following a possessive noun or pronoun. An initial article should also be omitted if another article or an adjective precedes it.

They planned on reading Tolkien's *Lord of the Rings* aloud. [*The* omitted]
The controversial *Charismatics* by John MacArthur [*The* omitted]

9. When specific words within run-in or block quotations are italicized for emphasis, the reader should be notified. An ascription, such as *italics mine* or *emphasis added*, should be placed in parentheses immediately after the quotation.

Note the contrast in David's parallelism: "When *we* were over-whelmed by sins, *you* forgave our transgressions" (Psalm 65:3, italics mine).

10. Names of modern versions of Scripture are set in italics, unlike the names of important historical versions of the Bible, which are set in roman type.

the Breeches Bible   *The Jerusalem Bible*
the King James Version   *The New King James Version*
The New International Version   the Vulgate

B. Small Caps

1. Small caps are commonly used for such abbreviations as A.D., B.C., A.M., P.M., MS, and MSS.

2. Abbreviations of translations and versions of Scripture are usually set in small caps (see the list on pages 115–18). Care must be exercised in distinguishing when a translator's, editor's, or paraphraser's name is being used as an abbreviation for a particular version (and therefore set in small caps) and when it refers to the person (and therefore set in regular type).

Most American writers abbreviate the name of the 1611 Bible as the KJV instead of the AV.
Their favorite modern paraphrase is PHILLIPS.
The small-group leader read from Phillips's paraphrase of Scripture.

3. To indicate who is speaking, small caps are used for the names of speakers in plays, dialogues, transcriptions of court-room proceedings, and other dramatic representations of conversations. Note that the first letter of such names is usually set in regular type.

EVERYMAN: O Jesu, help! All hath forsaken me.
GOOD DEEDS: Nay, Everyman; I will bide with thee.

4. Some book designs call for small caps to be used for the opening word (after an initial capital), phrase, or sentence

at the beginning of a chapter. Unless otherwise noted by the designer, all punctuation marks and all capital letters should remain in regular type.

PHILLIP BLISS'S HYMNS WERE POPULAR AT D. L. MOODY'S CAMPAIGNS.

5. Smalls caps may be used to indicate an accented syllable in informal renderings of phonetic pronunciation.

Eusebius (pronounced you-SEE-bee-us) is considered the father of church history.

C. Possessives

1. Most common singular nouns form the possessive by adding 's. Exceptions are made for a few common phrases that, perhaps for the sake of euphony, have come to require an apostrophe only. Plural possessives are formed by adding an apostrophe only, except for words whose plurals do not end in s. In those cases, the plural possessive is formed by adding 's to the word.

Remember Henry Ward Beecher's remark: All words are pegs to hang ideas on.
For conscience' sake, Baxter allied himself with the Nonconformists.
Parishioners' complaints did not hinder Susannah Wesley's evangelism.
At first the disciples did not believe the women's story.

2. As a rule, proper nouns form their possessives in the same way as common nouns, even when the proper noun ends in an s. When in doubt, euphony and common pronunciation should be your guides. For instance, when you would not ordinarily pronounce an extra possessive s, then only an apostrophe should be added in the written form.

Bliss's hymns   the Lewises' letters
John's gospel   John Rogers' Bible

3. Determining the possessive forms for classical and biblical names ending in *s* is often a problem. No system is perfect, but euphony and common pronunciation should be adhered to. When the possessive *s* is ordinarily pronounced, add *'s*; if it is awkward to pronounce the possessive *s*, then add an apostrophe only. The following rules should help. When the *s* represents the sound *z* at the end of the word (as in *Socrates* or *Thales*) or when the final *s* is immediately preceded by another *s* or *z* sound (as in *Augustus*, *Xerxes*, or *Jesus*), then only an apostrophe should be added. When the *s* represents an *s* sound and is not immediately preceded by another *s* or *z* sound (as in *Cyrus*), then *'s* should be added to form the possessive. Also, any classical or biblical name that is also a common modern name (like *James*), whether it ends in an *s* or a *z* sound, should form its possessive by adding *'s*.

Ananias's house	Thales' philosophy
Jesus' disciples	Thomas's doubt
Ramses' dynasty	Zacchaeus's tree

4. The names for feast days of saints are formed with the possessive.

All Saints' Day	Saint Patrick's Day
Saint Michael's Eve	Saint Valentine's Day

5. A possessive ending to an italicized noun should be set in roman.

John Timmer explains how the riches of the kingdom can be found in the *anawim*'s very poverty.
Sandy joined the *Banner*'s staff in 1980.

6. When a possessive needs to be formed for two or more persons in the same context, the following rules apply: (1) If one object is possessed mutually by all the people listed, then only the final name needs to be in a possessive form; (2) if separate objects are possessed, then each name should be in the possessive form. In some cases,

rewriting may be called for if the distinctions are not otherwise clear.

Keil and Delitzsch's study [the book they wrote together]
Vaughan's and Herbert's poetry [their separate poetry]
my aunt's and uncle's books [their separate books]
my aunt's books and my uncle's books [rewritten]

7. Phrases or epithets may form possessives as long as they are not more than three or four words in length and no ambiguity results. Otherwise, the sentence should be rewritten.

the Evil One's devices
the Good Shepherd's promises
the Apostle to the Gentile's writings [ambiguous]
the writings of the Apostle to the Gentiles [rewritten]

8. The plural possessive form is used when an object is described by the group of people that commonly use it, even though the idea of possession may not be implied. The singular possessive form is used when only one person commonly uses the object. Note also that it is common for many groups and organizations to drop the possessive form in their official names or functions; in these cases, adhere to the group's preference.

the nurses' station   cashier's table
writers' guidelines   Michigan Teachers Association
treasurer's office   Christian Booksellers Convention

D. Quotations

1. Authors are responsible to see that quotations are reproduced in wording, spelling, capitalization, and punctuation exactly as they appear in the original printed sources.

2. An initial letter may be changed to a capital or a lowercase letter, and a final punctuation mark may be changed to suit the syntax of the text. In older works, idiosyncrasies of spelling and capitalization should be observed; the word *sic*, enclosed in brackets, may be used

after an obvious misspelling but should be used sparingly. If the spelling or punctuation has been modernized, a general note should inform the reader that this has been done.

3. A short quotation may be run into the text (called a *run-in quotation*). A longer quotation is set off from the text (a *block quotation*) and is usually set in a smaller type size and with a narrower width. Generally a prose quotation of more than eight typed lines (or five or six typeset lines) should be set as a block quotation. Also, two or more lines of poetry are usually set as a block quotation.

4. When a block quotation is introduced by a word or phrase like *thus* or *the following*, that word or phrase should be followed by a colon. When a verb-of-saying introduces the block quotation, a comma is used. If it is introduced by a complete statement, then a period should be used. When the introductory phrase forms a grammatically complete unit with the block quotation that follows it, no punctuation should be used. Usually the syntax of the introductory phrase will suggest the correct punctuation.

> The role of the pastor has been described thus: [. . .]
> In his letter to Queen Ethelberga, Pope Boniface said, [. . .]
> O'Connor tells the legend of St. Francis and the wolf of Gubbio. [. . .]
> William Jay said in his book on prayer that [. . .]

5. The source of a block quotation may be credited in a footnote, an endnote, or a parenthetical reference after the quotation. In some cases, as in epigraphs, a dash may be used to inform the reader of the source.

> I went very unwillingly to a society in Aldersgate Street, where one was reading Luther's preface to the Epistle to the Romans. About a quarter before nine, while he was describing the change which God works in the heart through faith in Christ, I felt my heart strangely warmed.
> —John Wesley, *Journals*

6. It is the author's responsibility to make sure that quoted poetry is indented line for line as in the original.

7. When poetry, verse, or song lyrics are set as block quotations, they should be centered on the page according to the width of the longest line.

> All people that on earth do dwell,
>   Sing to the Lord with cheerful voice;
> Him serve with fear, His praise forth tell,
> Come ye before Him and rejoice.
>   — Hopkins, "The Old Hundreth"

8. Sometimes the question of tense arises with verbs-of-saying used with quotations. In most cases, logic and the context will dictate the tense. When in doubt, the best rule is this: an author spoke or wrote the work in the past, but the work itself speaks to us in the present.

> Solomon said, "Remember your creator in the days of your youth" (Ecclesiastes 12:1).
>
> As Ecclesiastes says, "Remember your creator in the days of your youth" (12:1).

E. Quotations from Scripture

In addition to the rules given for general quotations, some special rules should be specifically applied when quoting Scripture.

1. Familiar phrases from Scripture need not be set off by quotation marks or referenced.

> We too can share the shepherds' wonder at hearing the good tidings of great joy.

2. If, when quoting Scripture, the author needs to change an occasional word for clarity's sake, brackets are used to indicate the change.

> "We love because [God] first loved us" (1 John 4:19).

3. The author may wish to change a particular word or words of a given translation throughout an entire manuscript. This may be done without brackets as long as a general note informing the reader of this change is given in the front matter or on the copyright page. For instance, an author may want to replace the words *thee*, *thou*, *thy*, and *thine* of the King James Version with *you* and *your*. A note informing the reader of this change should be provided. This is also useful if the author wishes to change the capitalization style of the deity pronouns in the predominant translation used.

4. In most cases, ellipsis points should not be placed before or after a Scripture verse or a portion of a verse. If the quoted portion is a sentence fragment and might be confusing to the reader, then ellipsis points should be used. An introductory word such as *And*, *Or*, *For*, *Therefore*, *But*, *Verily*, and so on may be omitted from a Scripture verse without ellipsis points.

   "The God of all comfort . . . comforts us in all our troubles, so that we can comfort those in any trouble" (2 Cor. 1:3–4).

   "He that is not against us is on our part" (Mark 9:40 kjv). [The original reads: "For he that is not against us is on our part."]

5. In some versions of Scripture, the words *Lord* and *God* appear in capitals and small caps (LORD, GOD). In books written in a familiar or popular vein, this cap-and-small-cap style need not be followed. In scholarly works, however, quotations from Scripture should reflect the typographical rendering of the version cited.

6. Words that are italicized in the King James Version should not be italicized when quoted. The translators of the KJV used italics to indicate supplied words that did not have exact parallels in the original Greek or Hebrew. Since they were not intended for emphasis, these italicized words would only confuse the modern reader. The *New American Standard Bible* sets Old Testament quotes, when quoted in the New Testament, in capitals and small

capitals, and it also follows the KJV device of setting supplied words in italics. When quoting from the NASB, all cap-and-small-cap quotations and italicized words should be rendered in regular text type.

7. The KJV and some other versions provide pronunciation marks with proper names. These marks, of course, should not be reproduced when quoting from that version.

8. Some versions, most notably the KJV, set each verse as if it were a separate paragraph. Since this is merely a typographic convention, these verses, when quoted, should not be set as separate paragraphs. The actual paragraph breaks are indicated by the symbol ¶.

9. In text, biblical proper nouns should follow the spelling of the primary Scripture version used. When no primary translation is used, this manual recommends that proper nouns should follow the style given in the *New International Version*.

Ezekias [KJV]   Jehoshaphat [NIV]
Hezekiah [NIV]   Josaphat [KJV]

10. Because of the limitations of many typesetting systems, vowel ligatures should be set as separate letters when quoting from Bible versions that use such ligatures. Ligatures tend to look antiquated and may cause confusion.

F. Hyphenation

1. To answer questions about word division, the hyphenation of compound words, and other uses of the hyphen, this manual recommends *Webster's Ninth New Collegiate Dictionary* as an authoritative and accessible standard. Because of their frequent revision, college editions of dictionaries, like *Webster's New Collegiate*, tend to include newer words and a more current hyphenation style than unabridged editions. In many instances an author

must use personal discretion in hyphenating, and editorial staffs commonly adopt additional words as they gain currency. Only the most basic rules of hyphenation are given here. Because of the wide variety of hyphenated forms, chapter 6 and table 6.1 (pages 176–79) in CMS will prove helpful and should be consulted frequently.

2. When two or more words form an adjectival unit (compound adjective) preceding a noun, hyphens are placed between the words. When the compound adjective is used in a predicate form, it is set with no hyphens. Since some familiar compound adjectives are always hyphenated, it is best to check the dictionary.

R. A. Torrey's well-timed anecdote was effective.
R. A. Torrey's effective anecdote was well timed. [predicate; no hyphen]
The nineteenth-century liturgy sounded strange to our ears; it seemed so old-fashioned. [old-fashioned is always hyphenated]

3. An adverb ending in -ly never takes a hyphen when combined with an adjective.

a badly needed reform
a highly effective testimony

4. Hyphenation frequently depends on the syntactical use of a phrase or expression.

Is he born again? [predicate adjective]
Is he a born-again Christian? [adjective]
Soulwinning is not a negotiable duty of the Christian life. [noun]
Graham's inspired soul-winning sermons reached many. [adjective]

5. Many common prefixes and suffixes do not use hyphens, although *Webster's* should always be checked for exceptions. Among the prefixes and suffixes that do not commonly use hyphens are *anti-, co-, non-, out-, over-, post-, pre-, pseudo-, re-, semi-,* and *super-,* and *-fold* and *-like.* Keep in mind, though, that if confusion will result, or if a prefix is added to a proper name, a proper adjective

or noun, or a numeral, then a hyphen should be used.
Also use a hyphen if the added prefix or suffix results in a
double vowel (unless the word already appears in *Webster's* without the hyphen).

anti-intellectual	postwar
antimonarchic	pre-established
childlike	preexist [*Webster's*]
coauthor	pre-1939
coworker	pre-Reformation
non-Christian	prewar
nonviolent	reelect [*Webster's*]
out-Herod Herod	re-enumerate [double vowel]
outperform	threefold

6. The main exceptions to the previous rule are the prefixes
    all-, *ex-* (meaning former), *half-*, and *self-*, which gener-
    ally use hyphens unless the word is listed otherwise in
    Webster's.

all-faiths meeting	half-pint
all-weather arena	half-smile
ex-missionary	halfway [*Webster's*]
ex-pastor	self-sacrifice

7. Keep in mind that the meanings of some words will
    change depending on the insertion or deletion of a
    hyphen.

    They worked to recover the ministry's losses.
    They worked to re-cover the pews.
    God, in essence, brings about a re-creation of his chruch.
    We need recreation to refresh ourselves.

8. When two nouns of equal importance are temporarily
    yoked, they should be hyphenated. It should be empha-
    sized that the use of a solidus (slash) is incorrect.

    poet-priest   pastor-father   parent-guardian

9. Ideally, typeset words broken at the ends of lines should
    follow the rules for word division given in CMS (sections
    6.33–6.47). The exigencies of phototypesetting, however,

often make this difficult. Therefore, especially in later proof stages, it may be more economical to accept the word divisions from any major dictionary. (For more detail, see the advice for proofreaders on pages 167–68 of this manual.)

G. Outlining

1. Outlines should follow this style:

   I. C. S. Lewis
      A. Writings
         1. Fiction
            a. The *Narnia* books
               (1) *The Lion, the Witch and the Wardrobe*
                  (a) Characters
                     (i) Aslan

2. Runover lines should begin under the first letter of the first word in the previous line.

   1. Gregory contributes his support and energies to the formation of the Papal states.
   2. Gregory becomes a leading advocate of the missionary work in England.
   3. Taken as a whole, Gregory's writings earn him the status of "Doctor of the Church."
      a. *The Book of Morals* is his most extensive commentary.
      b. To this day, his *Dialogues* continue to be considered his most influential work.

3. Each level of an outline must have at least two points. In popular books where outlining is minimal, less formal, or not carried beyond the third level, it is acceptable to begin the outline with A. or 1., rather than the roman numeral.

H. Greek and Hebrew Transliterations

Various systems are used for transliterating Hebrew and Greek. The following chart should be helpful in most cases.

Greek

α = a	η = ē	ν = n	τ = t
β = b	θ = th	ξ = x	υ = y
γ = g	ι = i	o = o	φ = ph
δ = d	κ = k	π = p	χ = ch
ε = e	λ = l	ρ = r	ψ = ps
ζ = z	μ = m	σ,ς = s	ω = ō

αυ = au	γγ = ng	ᾳ = ā	ʿ = h
ευ = eu	γκ = nk	ῃ = ē	ῥ = rh
ηυ = ēu	γξ = nx	ῳ = ō	
ου = ou	γχ = nch		
υι = ui			

Hebrew

א = '	ד = d	י = y	ס = s	ר = r
ב = b	ה = h	כ = k	ע = ʿ	שׂ = ś
ב = b	ו = w	כ ך = k	פ = p	שׁ = š
ג = g	ז = z	ל = l	ף פ = p	ת = t
ג = g	ח = ḥ	מ ם = m	צ = ṣ	ת = t
ד = d	ט = ṭ	נ ן = n	ק = q	

(ה) ָ = â (h)	ָ = ā	ַ = a	ֳ = ᵃ
ְי = ê	ֵ = ē	ֶ = e	ֵ = e
ִי = î	ֹ = ō	ִ = i	ְ = e (if vocal)
וֹ = ô	ָ = o	ֻ = u	ֳ = o
וּ = û			

I. Gender-Specific Language

The growing awareness of subtle sexist messages in language requires that writers and editors develop a sensitivity to words and their overtones. They should strive for accurate, unbiased communication and avoid debasing terms, stereotypes, and language that expresses an inherent predominance of one sex over the other. Not only are the words themselves important, but so is the overall tone of a passage. The following guidelines can help writers and editors be more sensitive to sexist language so that they might affirm through words and attitudes the worth of all people.

1. Wording and phrasing should be neutral (impartial) when the sex of persons is unknown, immaterial, or consisting of both male and female. Good substitutes may be difficult to devise, but seldom impossible. Attempts at avoiding gender-specific language must improve communication and not result in awkwardness, inexactness, or obscurity.

2. The use of *man* to indicate both men and women is generally regarded as giving men predominance and should be avoided.

man, mankind	use:	humanity, people, human beings, humankind
the common man		the average person, the ordinary citizen
manhood		maturity, adulthood
spokesman		spokesperson, representative
chairman		chairperson, the chair
forefathers		forerunners, ancestors, precursors

3. Many vocational terms unnecessarily focus on gender and should be avoided.

fireman	use:	firefighter
steward, stewardess		flight attendant
pressman		press operator

foreman	supervisor
watchman	guard
housewife	homemaker, consumer
insurance man	insurance agent

4. Use neutral pronouns instead of the generic *he* whenever possible. Changing a phrase or recasting an entire sentence usually yields an acceptable alternative. One solution, which only works in some cases, might be to alternate non-gender-specific pronouns as they are needed in different contexts. Sometimes changing the pronouns from the singular to the plural remedies the problem. The following examples demonstrate problems and solutions:

Λ Christian needs to be concerned about his witness before the watching world. [*Problem:* the neutral subject *Christian* is followed by the male pronoun *his*.]

Λ Christian needs to be concerned about his or her witness before the watching world. [Acceptable, although *his or her* is awkward.]

Christians need to be concerned about their witness before the watching world. [Acceptable.]

5. Avoid double-standard semantics, such as describing a behavior as acceptable for one sex but not for the other. Connotations as well as denotations must be carefully considered.

authoritative husband, domineering wife
thrifty woman, miserly man
timid woman, spineless man
aggressive businessman, pushy businesswoman

6. Select words carefully to indicate gender. Many widely used terms have negative overtones and should not be used in fine writing. (By the same token, be selective about the words used to describe the elderly and people of various ethnic and racial backgrounds.)

| ladies, girls, gals | *use:* | women |
| lady, girl, gal | | woman |

old maid, spinster	single woman
the little woman, my better half	wife, spouse
women's libber	feminist
my old man	my husband, spouse
little old lady	elderly woman
dirty old man, little old man	elderly man

7. Do not hide gender if it is significant for the reader.

8. Do not violate essential rules of grammar.

9. In certain works that do not allow for reediting, such as reprints of classics or other previously published works, it may be advisable to place a disclaimer somewhere in the front matter, perhaps on the copyright page. This could state, for instance, that the publisher intends no sexist bias when masculine pronouns are used for a general reference.

J. Using *Webster's*

Webster's Third New International Dictionary and the useful desk reference, *Webster's Ninth New Collegiate Dictionary*, are descriptive rather than prescriptive dictionaries; that is, they list words in common use without making strict judgments as to which are or are not acceptable.

The editors of these dictionaries have also listed the definitions of each word according to historical sequence, so that the first definition for any given word is the usually oldest and not necessarily the most common. For writers and editors to agree on matters of consistent spelling, meaning, and capitalization, this manual recommends a few rules in the use of these dictionaries:

1. When alternative spellings are given, use the first. In some cases, the editors of the dictionary list the preferred alternative first; in other cases, all the alternatives are so common that they are simply listed alphabetically. In

either case, the principal of the "first alternative" should resolve most inconsistencies.

2. Use spellings given in main entries only. Do not use spellings from alternative entries that are followed by such phrases as *var of* (variant of).

3. In most cases, do not use words whose definitions or spellings are qualified by such terms as *archaic*, *nonstand* (nonstandard), *obs* (obsolete), *slang*, or *substand* (substandard).

4. Unless otherwise specified by the publisher's manual of style, capitalize all words marked *cap* (capitalize) or *usu cap* (usually capitalized), but lowercase all words marked *sometimes cap* (sometimes capitalized). Words marked *often cap* (often capitalized) should be capitalized or lowercased according to preference, usage, and common sense.

K. A Spelling and Capitalization List of Common Words

adviser
air force, the
Air Force, U.S.
anti-Communist (n.)
anticommunist (adj.)
anti-Zionist
army, the
Army, U.S.
appendixes
  (*not* appendices)
Asian (preferred to Oriental)
audiotape

backward
benefited
best-seller (n.)
best-selling (adj.)

Bible study (n. and adj.)
black (racial designation)
born-again (adj.)
boyfriend
businesspeople
businessperson

café
canceled
catalog
Communism
Communist (n.)
communist (adj.)
communistic
conservatism
conservative
copy editing

copy editor
counseled
counseling

Daddy, Dad
  (direct address)
daddy, dad
  (indirect reference)
Dark Ages, the
Depression, the
diagramed
  but diagrammable
disc (phonograph record)
disk (computer)

East Coast
entrée

façade
far-out
fiancé
fiancée
footwashing
free world
fulfillment
full-time (adj.)
fullness

girlfriend
glamour
good-bye
Gothic (style of art or type)
gothic novel
gray
Greater Chicago
grown-up (n. and adj.)

hang-up (n.)
hangout (n.)
Hispanic (preferred to Latin
  American)

Holocaust (when referring to
  Nazi atrocities against Jews)
homeland
hometown

indexes (not indices)
Iron Curtain
italic type

kidnapped
kidnapper
kidnapping
kindergarten
kindergartner

labeled
latchkey child
Latin American (see Hispanic)
layman, laymen
layperson, laypeople
laywoman, laywomen
liberal
liberalism
lifestyle
life's work
loanword

maître d'
marines
Marines, U.S.
medieval
middle-aged (adj.)
Middle Ages, the
Midwest, midwestern
mindset
Mommy, Mom (direct address)
mommy, mom (indirect
  reference)
Muhammad
Muslim

naïve
native American
navy
Navy, U.S.
New World
New Year's Day

okay
Old World
Oriental (see *Asian*)

part-time
peacemaking
percent
proofreader
proof text

Renaissance
restroom
résumé
Roman numeral
roman type
roommate

skeptic
South (Civil War)
Southwest

storytelling
Sunday school (n. and adj.)

teenage, teenager
Third World
timeline
totaled
toward (no final *s*)
traveling, traveled
twentieth century

unchristian
uptight

videotape
Vietnam, Vietnamese

way-out
West Coast
whiskey
white (racial designation)
woolly
wordplay
word processor
worldview
worshiped, worshiper, worshiping

L. Commonly Misspelled Words

In the following list, an asterisk (*) indicates those words that are common in religious works. The underscores show the common problem spots; that is, those letters that are often mistakenly dropped or replaced with other letters.

abscess
accidentally
accommodate

achieve
acknowledgment
algae

allotted
all right
analogous

annihilate
anoint*
archaeology
argument

banister
barbiturate
battalion
beggar
belligerent
bizarre
bouillon
broccoli
burglar

Cadillac
caffeine
calendar
camaraderie
canister
caress
Caribbean
catalyst
cemetery
chauffeur
colonnade
Colosseum
commitment
computer
confetti
connoisseur
consensus
coolly
crystal

deductible
defendant
demagogue
dependent
despicable
diarrhea

dilettante
discipline
dissect
drunkenness

ecstasy
embarrass
entrepreneur
entrust
erratic
eunuch
exalt (lift up)
exhilarate
existence
extension
exult (rejoice)

fluorescent
foreign
foresee
fulfill
fuselage

genealogy
government
grammar
guerrilla
guttural
gynecologist
gypsy

hangar (for airplanes)
harass
hemorrhage
holistic

inadvertent
indispensable
innate
innocuous
inoculate

iridescent
irrelevant
irresistible

judgment (no e)

liaison
license
lightning
limousine
liquefy

machete
maintenance
manageable
maneuver
mannequin
margarine
marshal
mercenary
millennium*
minuscule
miscellaneous
misspell
moustache

necessary
newsstand
nickel
niece

occasion
occurrence

pallid
parallel
paraphernalia
parishioners*
pastime
perseverance

pharaoh*
phlegm
Philippians*
Philippines
picnicking
pistachio
pneumonia
Portuguese
prairie
precede
preferring
prerogative
presumptuous
principally
privilege
proceed
prophecy (n.)
prophesy (v.)
publicly (not -ally)

questionnaire

rarefied
raspberry
recommendation
repentance
repetition
resistance
restaurateur (no n)
rhythm
ridiculous

sacrilegious*
scurrilous
seize
separate
sergeant
sheriff
siege
sieve
skillful
spigot
subpoena

supersede

temperamental
timbrel
tonsillitis
totally
toxin
tranquillity
tyranny

vacuum
vengeance
vilify

weird
wholly

yield

zephyr

M. Commonly Misspelled Proper Names

Certain names common to religious books, especially those names that use accents, can cause problems. Note the spellings, alphabetical order, accents, and particles of the following:

Lancelot Andrewes
Thomas à Becket
Gerrit Berkouwer
Dietrich Bonhoeffer
Frederick Buechner
André Bustanoby
Andraé Crouch
Teilhard de Chardin
Carmen Bernos de Gasztold
Catherine de Hueck

François Fénelon
John Foxe
Glaphré
Madame (Mme.) Guyon
Dag Hammarskjöld
Søren Kierkegaard
Hans Küng
Tim and Beverly LaHaye
George MacDonald
George Müller

Reinhold Niebuhr
Francis Schaeffer
Corrie ten Boom (*but* the
  Ten Boom family)

Thomas à Kempis
J. R. R. Tolkien
Susanna Wesley
John Wycliffe

N. Miscellaneous Notes on Usage

This manual cannot attempt to address the many complexities of English usage. The following points only highlight a few terms that are commonly used in religious books. While other notes on usage appear throughout this manual, only those that have not been discussed elsewhere are listed here.

1. Since A.D. stands for *anno Domini* ("the year of the Lord"), it was once considered improper to use the abbreviation with any but single-year references. It has now become acceptable, however, to use A.D. with century designations as well, in which case the abbreviation follows the date.

   A.D. 90 *but* the first century A.D.

2. *Agnostic* and *atheist* should not be used synonymously. An agnostic is one who says, in effect, "I don't know whether a divine being exists." An atheist says, "A divine being does not exist."

3. The word *catholic*, when lowercased, means "universal, or general." When capitalized, it refers to the Roman Catholic Church.

4. Care must be exercised in using the word *charismatic*. In the broadest sense it means "personally attractive and compelling." In the stricter and more religious sense, it has come to mean "characterized by an emphasis upon the gifts of the Holy Spirit."

5. *Episcopal* is an adjective; *Episcopalian* is the noun.

   The Episcopalian spoke with the Episcopal minister.

6. Although accepted in most dictionaries, the words *help-meet* and *helpmate* are best reserved for informal or colloquial contexts, based as they are on a misreading of Genesis 2:18 (KJV): "I will make him an help meet for him." *Meet*, in this case, means "suitable," not "mate." Also, the terms are now archaic.

7. *InterVarsity.* To allay confusion, the publisher and the Christian organization that go by that name in the U.S. have recently standardized its spelling. Thus: InterVarsity Press and InterVarsity Christian Fellowship. The organization that goes by that name in the British Isles, however, spells the word with a hyphen: Inter-Varsity.

8. In the United States, the term *King James Version (KJV)* is preferred to *Authorized Version (AV)* in references to the 1611 Bible commissioned by James I of England. *Authorized Version* is used primarily in the United Kingdom and its commonwealth.

9. The terms *layperson* and *laypeople* have replaced the older terms *layman* and *laymen* as non-gender-specific terms. The term *laity* also refers to both men and women. *Laymen* and *laywomen* are best used when it is important to specify that a group of laypeople consists entirely of members of one sex or the other.

10. The term *Muslim* is preferred to *Moslem*. Also, the preferred form of the name of the founder of Islam is *Muhammad*, not *Mohammad* or *Mahomet*.

11. Because of its association with the parable of the prodigal son, the word *prodigal* is mistakenly thought to mean "wandering" or "straying." The word, in fact, means "wasteful" and "excessive," and should be used to convey those meanings. To refer to a runaway child as a prodigal is only true if that child has indulged in wasteful excesses.

12. Be careful to distinguish between *prophecy* (a noun) and *prophesy* (a verb).

    A false prophet may prophesy, but will his prophecy come to pass?

13. The title *reverend* is often misused in writing and conversation. In precise writing, it is comparable to the title *honorable*; both words should be accompanied by the article *the*, and neither word should be used with a last name alone. In informal contexts, the article may be dropped, although this is considered colloquial. The use of the word *reverend* as a noun is also quite colloquial and should be avoided in formal writing since the word is properly an adjective. These colloquial uses are best reserved for dialogue.

> Many listeners have been touched by the Reverend Gary Davis's songs.
> He introduced Reverend Wilkins to us. [colloquial; not for formal writing]
> "We spoke to the reverend about our marriage plans." [dialogue]

14. The plural of *shofar*, the ram's horn trumpet used on Jewish holidays, is *shofroth*.

15. The abbreviation *Xmas* for Christmas should not be used in formal writing. It is appropriate only for advertising copy. Oddly enough, the abbreviation has a long and established history in English, dating back to the sixteenth century. The X is actually the Greek letter *chi* and has been used as a symbol for the name of Christ (Christos) since the first century.

16. Christians have developed a vocabulary that may or may not be understandable to non-Christians. While many of these words and phrases are essential to clear writing, writers should be wary of Christian jargon. Unconsciously, some authors have allowed the rhetorical language of sermons, hymns, and devotional literature to shape their prose, resulting in indefiniteness, lack of originality, and at worst, insincerity. Here are a few clichés to avoid:

abundant life
after God's own heart
believe on (the name of the Lord)
born again
burden on my heart
carnal desires
Christian walk
daily walk
den of iniquity
depths of depravity
depths of despair
desires of the flesh
devout Catholic
epitome of evil
eternal refuge
eternal resting place
eternal reward
fervent prayer
forever and ever
from on high
get into the Word
giant of the faith
God-fearing man [or woman]
God made known to me
God revealed to me
God-shaped vacuum
good Christian
groanings of the spirit
grounded in the faith
grounded in the Word
heart of the gospel
heavenly angels
heavenly anthems
hellfire and damnation
hopeless sinner
inspired Word of God
just pray (just ask)
laid upon my heart
let go and let God

life-changing experience
life everlasting
life of sin
lift up the Lord
lift [someone] up in prayer
lusts of the flesh
meet his [or her] Maker
moved by the Spirit
of old [as in "Abraham of old"]
passions of the flesh
pearly gates
prayer warrior
precious blood of Jesus
prepare our hearts
primrose path
realms of glory
rooted in the faith
rooted in the Word
saving knowledge of Christ
seventh heaven
share a verse [of Scripture]
sins of the fathers
snares of the Devil
sorely tempted
soul of humility
soul-stirring message
spiritual high
spiritual state
spoke to my heart
stand before the judgment seat
stars in one's crown
storms [tempests] of life
straight and narrow
take it to the Lord
throughout eternity
time immemorial
traveling mercies
trials and tribulations
trophies of grace

trust and obey
unto eternity
unspoken needs
uphold in prayer
urgings of the spirit
vale of tears
victorious living

walk with God
watch and pray
wicked ways
wiles of the Devil
wondrous ways of God
word of prayer

V.
NUMBERS

A. General Use of Numbers

1. Spell out numbers under one hundred and round numbers in hundreds, thousands, millions, billions, etc. Extremely large round numbers may be expressed in figures and units of millions or billions. Numerals should be used for all other numbers.

thirty-four	two million	2.4 billion
fifteen hundred	1,876	195

2. The above rule also applies to ordinal numbers. In notes, tabular matter, and a few traditional expressions, a combination of numeral and suffix is used, without periods. The abbreviation of *second* and *third* are *2d* and *3d*, not *2nd* and *3rd*.

tenth grade	38th parallel
twentieth century	*Words Into Type*, 3d edition

3. In literary, limited, or informal use, numbers should be spelled out for percentages. For technical or statistical use, numerals should be used for percentages. Numerals should be used with all decimal fractions and mathematical or scientific symbols and references.

   He graduated in the top ten percent of his class. [informal use]

The poll showed that only 10 percent of the people in that denomination believed in the Virgin Birth. [statistical use]

a 3.9 average   32° F
4.2 billion people   3 + 4 = 7
240 volts   5'6"

4. To indicate dimensions, numbers are spelled out or set as numerals according to the context. The symbol × or the letter x may replace the word "by" in technical works, but is discouraged in nontechnical writing.

three-by-five card *or* 3 x 5 card
8½-by-11-inch paper

5. Use numerals for numbers referring to parts of a book.

The author makes three points in chapter 6, as indicated in table 3 on page 97.

6. A number should be spelled out at the beginning of a sentence. If this is cumbersome, rewrite the sentence so that it does not begin with the number.

Nineteen seventy-eight marked the five-hundredth anniversary of the birth of Sir Thomas More.
The five-hundredth anniversary of the birth of Sir Thomas More was observed in 1978.

7. Except for year dates, most numbers should be spelled out in dialogue. Numerals may also be used in those cases in which numbers are so large that it would be impractical to spell them out.

"On October thirty-first, 1517," said the tour guide, "more than four hundred and fifty years ago, Luther affixed his Ninety-five Theses to this very door."

8. In figures of 1000 or more, commas should be used except in the numbers that indicate whole thousands of less than 10,000.

31,928   1000   9,500
1,476   9000   5,000,000

9. Monetary references should be spelled out or set in numerals according to the rules for numbers given in rule 1 on page 99. If many dollar amounts are given in close context, they should be set as numerals. When fractional and whole dollar amounts appear in close proximity to each other, zeroes should be placed after the decimals in the whole dollar amounts for consistency.

> Hundreds paid ten dollars each to hear Andraé Crouch in person.
> The deacons collected a total of $413.
> The agent received $9.50, $22.74, and $28.00 for the three sales.

10. Numbers indicating ages of persons should always be spelled out. Also note the correct hyphenation of the following forms.

> the five-year-olds
> a twenty-five-year-old woman
> he was sixty years old

11. If several numbers are given for several items in one general group, then all the numbers should be handled in the same way. If the largest contains three or more digits, use figures for all.

> With a choir of fifty people and a worship committee of more than thirty, why can we get only two people to take care of infants on Sunday?
> There are 14 graduate students in the religion department, 61 in the classics department, and 93 in the romance languages, making a total of 168 in the three departments.

12. In formal writing, streets that bear a number as the name should be spelled out. But house numbers or other numbers used in street addresses should always be given in figures.

> Fifth Avenue   21 Forty-second Street
> Fifty-second Street   221 Baker Street

13. To indicate that an entire range of numbers is being referred to, an unspaced en dash is used between the numbers. These are called *inclusive numbers*. The sec-

ond number may be elided (shortened) in many numbers, especially in year numerals and page references. Since the rules of elision are difficult to describe, the following examples should make them easier to grasp.

Years:
1900–1902 [do not elide when first number ends in 00]
1900–1911 [do not elide when first number ends in 00]
1904–8
1910–14
1905–13
1914–18
A.D. 374–379 [do not elide when used with A.D. or B.C.]

Page and other references:
2–3
22–23 [not 22–3]
100–107 [do not elide when first number ends in 00]
100–119 [do not elide when first number ends in 00]
101–5
110–25
151–58
1,081–87
but note the following: 12,483–12,515 *not* 12,483–515

B. Time and Dates

1. Times of day are usually spelled out unless an exact moment of time is emphasized, in which case figures are used.

   The evening service ended at about half-past seven.
   Sunday school begins at 9:30 sharp, and the worship service begins at 11:00.

2. The abbreviations A.M. and P.M. are usually set in small caps, although they are sometimes set in lowercase letters (a.m., p.m.). In either case, the style should be consistent throughout a project. The words *morning, evening,* and *o'clock* should never be combined with the designations A.M. or P.M.

10:45 in the morning   4:00 P.M.
10:45 A.M.   four o'clock in the afternoon

3. References to millennia, centuries, and decades should
   be spelled out. If numerals are used for decades, add an *s*
   with no apostrophe. In informal contexts the full number
   of a specific year is sometimes abbreviated with an
   apostrophe, as, for instance, with year designations for
   automobiles and for graduating classes.

second millennium B.C.   the 1740s
sixteenth century   a '57 Chevy
the seventies and eighties   the class of '84

4. Do not abbreviate the names of the months in running
   text, although they may be abbreviated in references or
   charts.

Jan.	Apr.	July	Oct.
Feb.	May	Aug.	Nov.
Mar.	June	Sept.	Dec.

5. Do not abbreviate days of the week in text. If a special
   situation calls for an abbreviation, use the following:

Sun.   Mon.   Tues.   Wed.   Thurs.   Fri.   Sat.

6. The abbreviations B.C. and A.D. are usually set in small
   caps with periods, although it is becoming common to see
   them set in standard caps with no periods (BC, AD),
   especially in popular works of history. Place A.D. before a
   specific year reference, although it should follow a
   reference to an entire century. The abbreviation B.C.
   always comes after a century or year reference.

A.D. 597   ninth century A.D.
55 B.C.   first century B.C.

7. Write complete dates in one of the following styles. The
   first is preferred for scholarly and reference works. Never
   use the ordinal abbreviations *st, d, nd, rd,* or *th* after
   figures in dates.

[Style 1:] Wesley's conversion took place on 24 May 1738.
[Style 2:] On May 30, 1934, the Barmen Declaration was signed.
[Style 3:] On the first day of September 1670, William Penn's trial began.
December 25, not December 25th

8. When a month or season designation is immediately followed by a year, a comma should not be used.

    William Booth's tent ministry in the East End began in July 1865.

9. Many historical references distinguish between dates from the Julian calendar and those from the Gregorian calendar by using the abbreviations O.S. (Old Style) and N.S. (New Style) respectively. Unless otherwise specified, most modern references are in New Style. The new calendar was established in 1582, although many Western countries did not adopt it until many years later. The Eastern Orthodox Church still dates its holidays by the older Julian calendar.

    Dates in and around the year in which a specific country adopted the Gregorian calendar should be checked carefully. For instance, when Great Britain and the American colonies adopted the New Style system in 1752, two important changes took place. First, eleven days were dropped from the calendar (the day after September 2, 1752, was considered September 14, 1752). Also, January 1 was officially made the first day of 1752, whereas before that time March 25 had traditionally been considered New Year's Day in England.

    In referring to years before 1752 in English history, dates between January 1 and March 24 are sometimes listed with a double-year designation. A solidus is used between the elided year numerals. Again, if no such designation is given, it can usually be assumed that a New Style date is being referred to.

    The storm at sea that lead to John Newton's conversion took place on March 21, N.S. (March 10, O.S.).
    The service took place on Epiphany, January 6, 1720/21.

10. In the Quaker system of dating, days and months are usually spelled out and lowercased. Also note that before 1752, the Quakers considered March the first month of the year.

> Nineteen-year-old George Fox left home on the ninth day, the seventh month, 1643. [September 9, 1643.]

C. Scripture References

1. Use Arabic rather than Roman numerals for books of the Bible. It is preferable to write out the number if it begins a sentence.

> 1 Corinthians, *not* I Corinthians
> First John 4:7 tells us . . .

2. When only a chapter is referred to, it may be spelled out, although a numeral may be used if no confusion will result.

> In the first chapter of Genesis . . . or In Genesis 1 . . .

3. Numerals may be used for Scripture references in dialogue, although frequently the syntax requires they be spelled out.

> "I'm sure," said the minister, "everyone here could recite John 3:16 by heart."
> "Amanda Smith overcame her fear by remembering the third chapter of Galatians and the twenty-eighth verse."

4. Names of the books of the Bible may be abbreviated when a reference is enclosed in parentheses, especially when such references are numerous. Otherwise, they should be abbreviated in text only in scholarly or reference works. See pages 111–15 for a complete list of abbreviations of books of the Bible.

5. The abbreviation for *verse* is *v.* and, for *verses*, *vv.* These abbreviations should be used in parenthetical references

only or when they are used so often in text as to make the spelled-out forms impractical.

Later in the eleventh chapter (v. 42) John wrote, "In that place many believed in Jesus."

VI.
ABBREVIATIONS

A. General Rules

1. Personal names should be abbreviated in accordance with the person's preference or with the form given in a competent authority, such as *Webster's New Biographical Dictionary*. Two or more initials should be separated by normal word spacing (or a three-point space), though they should not be allowed to break over line endings. If a person's initials are used as a nickname, then they should be set with no space between the letters.

   J. R. R. Tolkien *not* J.R.R. Tolkien
   P. J. Hoff *but* P.J.

2. As a rule, do not use abbreviations in dialogue. *Dr.*, *Mr.*, *Mrs.*, and *Ms.*, however, are always abbreviated.

3. Most authorities disapprove of the use of *Rev.* with a last name alone and also recommend that the abbreviation be used with the article *the*. Various other forms are permissible. (For a discussion of the use of the word *reverend*, see page 96.)

   the Rev. Billy Graham   Mr. Graham
   the Rev. Mr. Graham   *but not* Rev. Graham

4. Spell out a civil or military title in running text when used with a surname only. Abbreviate it if the full name is used.

Governor Wallace *but* Gov. Lew Wallace
General Booth *but* Gen. William Booth

5. In text, the names of corporations or organizations should be given in full, although the abbreviations *Inc.* and *Ltd.* are usually dropped.

6. When initials are used for the names of agencies and organizations, periods are usually not used. This also applies to famous persons referred to by initials only. Also, many abbreviated terms in biblical scholarship omit periods.

YMCA	JFK	Q
NATO	GKC	NT

7. The names of states, provinces, and countries should usually be spelled out in text. In lists, footnotes, indexes, bibliographies, or charts, state, province, and country names may be abbreviated with standard abbreviations. Two-letter postal abbreviations for states and provinces should be used only when actual mailing addresses are given. The following list shows state and province abbreviations in both standard and postal style.

Alabama	Ala.	AL
Alaska	Alaska	AK
Arizona	Ariz.	AZ
Arkansas	Ark.	AR
California	Calif.	CA
Colorado	Colo.	CO
Connecticut	Conn.	CT
Delaware	Del.	DE
Florida	Fla.	FL
Georgia	Ga.	GA
Hawaii	Hawaii	HI
Idaho	Ida.	ID
Illinois	Ill.	IL
Indiana	Ind.	IN
Iowa	Ia.	IA
Kansas	Kans.	KS

Kentucky	Ky.	KY
Louisiana	La.	LA
Maine	Me.	ME
Maryland	Md.	MD
Massachusetts	Mass.	MA
Michigan	Mich.	MI
Minnesota	Minn.	MN
Mississippi	Miss.	MS
Missouri	Mo.	MO
Montana	Mont.	MT
Nebraska	Neb.	NE
Nevada	Nev.	NV
New Hampshire	N.H.	NH
New Jersey	N.J.	NJ
New Mexico	N.Mex.	NM
New York	N.Y.	NY
North Carolina	N.C.	NC
North Dakota	N.Dak.	ND
Ohio	Ohio	OH
Oklahoma	Okla.	OK
Oregon	Ore.	OR
Pennsylvania	Pa.	PA
Rhode Island	R.I.	RI
South Carolina	S.C.	SC
South Dakota	S.Dak.	SD
Tennessee	Tenn.	TN
Texas	Tex.	TX
Utah	Utah	UT
Vermont	Vt.	VT
Virginia	Va.	VA
Washington	Wash.	WA
West Virginia	W.Va.	WV
Wisconsin	Wis.	WI
Wyoming	Wyo.	WY
Alberta	Alta.	AB
British Columbia	B.C.	BC
Manitoba	Man.	MB
New Brunswick	N.B.	NB
Newfoundland	Nfld.	NF
Northwest Territories	N.W.T.	NT

Nova Scotia	N.S.	NS
Ontario	Ont.	ON
Prince Edward Island	P.E.I.	PE
Quebec	Que. or P.Q.	QC
Saskatchewan	Sask.	SK
Yukon Territory	Y.T.	YT

8. Although most country names should be spelled out in text, the following common abbreviations are exceptions. Note that no space is used between the letters of these abbreviations.

Soviet Union—U.S.S.R.   United Kingdom—U.K.
United States—U.S.

9. No single rule governs the abbreviation of prefixes to geographical names. *Saint* is ordinarily abbreviated (*St.*) when it is used in place names but should be spelled out when used before the name of a person. *Mount* and *Fort* are preferred to *Mt.* and *Ft.*; *Point* and *Port* are always spelled out. Compass directions used as prefixes are spelled out.

St. Louis   Forth Worth   Port Huron
Mount Carmel   Point Barrow   West Chicago

10. The following list indicates how the elements of a book may be abbreviated in references or bibliographies. Except where noted, plurals of these abbreviations are formed by adding *s*.

appendix	app.	note(s)	n. (nn.)
bibliography	bibliog.	number	no.
book	bk.	page(s)	p. (pp.)
chapter	chap.	paragraph	par.
column	col.	part	pt.
figure	fig.	section	sec.
folio(s)	fol. (ff.)	verse(s)	v. (vv)
introduction	intro.	volume	vol.

11. Bibliographical abbreviations of important books and periodicals are often used in scholarly reference works. A

key to such abbreviations should appear in the front matter of the book. In such cases, the abbreviations are set without periods and in roman type. Usually the title of the work is abbreviated, but in some cases the authors' names are abbreviated instead. For certain well-known works, an editor's or author's last name can be a substitute for the actual title. Some common examples follow:

ANCL—*Ante-Nicene Christian Library*
BETS—*Bulletin of the Evangelical Theological Society*
CMS—*The Chicago Manual of Style*
KD—Keil and Delitzsch, *Commentary on the Old Testament*
ODCC—*The Oxford Dictionary of the Christian Church*
OED—*The Oxford English Dictionary*
Nestle—Nestle [editor], *Novum Testamentum Graece*
Trench—Trench [author], *Synonyms of New Testament Words*

B. Books of the Bible and Related Material

Books of the Bible, the Apocrypha, and pseudobiblical writings are generally spelled out in text, although they may be abbreviated in parenthetical references, especially when such references are numerous. Otherwise, they should be abbreviated in text only in scholarly or reference works. Two styles of abbreviation are recommended: a general style and a scholarly style. In deciding which style to use, the author and editor should keep the audience in mind. Note that some shorter names are not abbreviated at all. The Old and New Testament lists are based on the titles given in the *New International Version* of the Bible, but these should be adapted when a different title is given in another translation.

Title of Book	General Style	Scholarly Style
Old Testament		
Genesis	Gen.	Ge
Exodus	Ex.	Ex
Leviticus	Lev.	Lev
Numbers	Num.	Nu
Deuteronomy	Deut.	Dt

Title of Book	General Style	Scholarly Style
Joshua	Josh.	Jos
Judges	Judg.	Jdg
Ruth	Ruth	Ru
1 Samuel	1 Sam.	1Sa
2 Samuel	2 Sam.	2Sa
1 Kings	1 Kings	1Ki
2 Kings	2 Kings	2Ki
1 Chronicles	1 Chron.	1Ch
2 Chronicles	2 Chron.	2Ch
Ezra	Ezra	Ezr
Nehemiah	Neh.	Ne
Esther	Est.	Est
Job	Job	Job
Psalm(s)	Ps. (Pss.)	Ps(s)
Proverbs	Prov.	Pr
Ecclesiastes	Eccl.	Ecc
Song of Songs	Song	SS
Isaiah	Isa.	Isa
Jeremiah	Jer.	Jer
Lamentations	Lam.	La
Ezekiel	Ezek.	Eze
Daniel	Dan.	Da
Hosea	Hos.	Hos
Joel	Joel	Joel
Amos	Amos	Am
Obadiah	Obad.	Ob
Jonah	Jonah	Jnh
Micah	Mic.	Mic
Nahum	Nah.	Na
Habakkuk	Hab.	Hab
Zephaniah	Zeph.	Zep
Haggai	Hag.	Hag
Zechariah	Zech.	Zec
Malachi	Mal.	Mal

New Testament

Matthew	Matt.	Mt
Mark	Mark	Mk

Title of Book	General Style	Scholarly Style
Luke	Luke	Lk
John	John	Jn
Acts	Acts	Ac
Romans	Rom.	Ro
1 Corinthians	1 Cor.	1Co
2 Corinthians	2 Cor.	2Co
Galatians	Gal.	Gal
Ephesians	Eph.	Eph
Philippians	Phil.	Php
Colossians	Col.	Col
1 Thessalonians	1 Thess.	1Th
2 Thessalonians	2 Thess.	2Th
1 Timothy	1 Tim.	1Ti
2 Timothy	2 Tim.	2Ti
Titus	Titus	Tit
Philemon	Philem.	Phm
Hebrews	Heb.	Heb
James	James	Jas
1 Peter	1 Peter	1Pe
2 Peter	2 Peter	2Pe
1 John	1 John	1Jn
2 John	2 John	2Jn
3 John	3 John	3Jn
Jude	Jude	Jude
Revelation	Rev.	Rev

Apocrypha

1 Esdras	1 Esd.	1Es
2 Esdras	2 Esd.	2Es
Tobit	Tobit	Tb
Judith	Judith	Jth
The Rest of Esther	Rest of Est.	RE
The Wisdom of Solomon	Wisd. Sol.	WS
Ecclesiasticus	Ecclus.	Eccus
Baruch	Bar.	Bar
The Song of the Three Holy Children	S. of III Ch.	STHC

Title of Book	General Style	Scholarly Style
Susanna	Sus.	Sus
Bel and the Dragon	Bel	Bel
Prayer of Manasses	Pr. Man.	PrM
1 Maccabees	1 Macc.	1Mc
2 Maccabees	2 Macc.	2Mc

Pseudepigrapha

Assumption of Moses	As. Moses	AM
Syriac Apocalypse of Baruch	2 Bar.	2Ba
Greek Apocalypse of Baruch	3 Bar.	3Ba
Ethiopic Book of Enoch	1 Enoch	1En
Slavonic Book of Enoch	2 Enoch	2En
Hebrew Book of Enoch	3 Enoch	3En
4 Ezra	4 Ezra	4Ezr
Joseph and Asenath	Joseph	JA
Book of Jubilees	Jub.	Jub
Letter of Aristeas	L. Aris.	Aris
Life of Adam and Eve	Adam and Eve	Adam
Lives of the Prophets	Prophets	LP
Martyrdom and Ascension of Isaiah	Mar. and As. Isa.	MA Isa
3 Maccabees	3 Macc.	3Mc
4 Maccabees	4 Macc.	4Mc
Odes of Solomon	Odes Sol.	OS
Paralipomena of Jeremiah	Paralip.	PJ
Pirke Aboth	Pirke Aboth	PA
Psalm 151	Ps. 151	Ps 151
Psalms of Solomon	Pss. Sol.	PS
Sibylline Oracles	Sib. Oracles	Sib
Story of Ahikar	Ahikar	Ahi
Testament of Abraham	T. Abram.	TAb

Title of Book	General Style	Scholarly Style
Testament of Adam	T. Adam	TAd
Testament of Benjamin	T. Ben.	TBen
Testament of Dan	T. Dan	TDan
Testament of Gad	T. Gad	TGad
Testament of Job	T. Job	TJob
Testament of Joseph	T. Jos.	TJos
Testament of Levi	T. Levi	TLevi
Testament of Naphtali	T. Naph.	TNaph
Testaments of the Twelve Patriarchs	T. Pats.	TPat
Zadokite Fragments	Zad. Frag.	ZF

C. Bible Versions in English

AB	*The Anchor Bible* (1964)
ABUV	*American Bible Union Version* (1912)
ALFORD	*New Testament in Basic English* (Alford)
AMPLIFIED	*Amplified Bible* (1958–65)
ARV	American Revised Version (1901; U.S. edition of ERV)
ARV, mg	American Revised Version, margin
ASV	*American Standard Version* (1901)
AT	*The Complete Bible: An American Translation* (Goodspeed and Smith; NT 1923; OT 1927)
AV	Authorized Version (1611; same as KJV)
BARCLAY	*The New Testament* (Barclay; 1968–69)
BECK	*New Testament in Language of Today* (Beck; 1963)
BISHOP	The Bishop's Bible (1568)
BV	*Berkeley Version in Modern English* (NT 1945; OT 1959)
COVERDALE	Coverdale Bible (1535)

DV	Douay-Rheims Bible (same as Douay Version; 1609–10)
DV	Douay Version (1609–10)
EB	*Emphasized Bible* (Rotherham; NT 1897; OT 1902)
ERV	English Revised Version (NT 1881; OT 1885; Apoc. 1895; same as RV)
ERV, mg	English Revised Version, margin
GENEVA	Geneva Bible (1560)
GNB	*Good News Bible* (same as TEV; NT 1966; OT 1976)
GREAT	Great Bible (1539)
HNB	*Holy Name Bible* (1963)
HOOKE	*The Bible in Basic English* (Hooke; NT 1940; OT 1949)
JB	*Jerusalem Bible* (French 1956; English 1966)
JPS	*Holy Scriptures: Jewish Publication Society Version of the Old Testament* (1917)
KJII	*King James II Version* (1971)
KJV	King James Version (same as Authorized Version; 1611)
KNOX	*Holy Bible: A Translation from the Latin Vulgate in the Light of the Hebrew and Greek Original* (Knox; NT 1945; OT 1949)
LAMSA	*Holy Bible from Ancient Eastern Manuscripts* (Lamsa; 1957)
LATTIMORE	*The Four Gospels and the Revelation* (Lattimore; 1979); *Acts and Letters of the Apostles* (Lattimore; 1982)
LB	*The Living Bible* (NT 1967; OT 1971)
LB	*The Book* (same as *The Living Bible*)
MATTHEW	Matthew Bible (1537)
MLB	*Modern Language Bible* (same as *New Berkeley Version*; 1969)

MLB	*New Berkeley Version in Modern English* (same as *Modern Language Bible;* 1969)
MOFFAT	*A New Translation of the Bible* (Moffat; NT 1913; OT 1924)
MONTGOMERY	*Centenary Translation of the New Testament in Modern English* (Montgomery; 1924)
MOULTON	*Modern Reader's Bible* (Moulton; 1907)
NAB	*New American Bible* (NT 1941; OT 1969)
NASB	*New American Standard Bible* (NT 1963; OT 1971)
NEB	*New English Bible* (NT 1961; OT and Apoc. 1970)
NIV	*New International Version* (NT 1973; OT 1978)
NIVSB	*NIV Study Bible* (1985)
NJV	*New Jewish Version* (1962–82)
NKJV	*New King James Version* (1979)
NORLIE	*New Testament in Modern English* (Norlie; 1951)
NOYES	*The New Testament* (Noyes; 1868)
NSRB	*New Scofield Reference Bible* (KJV; 1967)
NWT	*New World Translation of the Holy Scriptures* (Jehovah's Witnesses; 1961)
OAB	*Oxford Annotated Bible* (RSV; 1962)
PHILLIPS	*New Testament in Modern English* (Phillips; 1958)
RDB	*Reader's Digest Bible* (condensed RSV; 1982)
RHEIMS	Rheims New Testament (NT of DV; 1582)
RIEU	*Penguin Bible* (Rieu; 1952)
RSV	*Revised Standard Version* (NT 1946; OT 1952; Apoc. 1957)
RV	Revised Version (NT 1881; OT 1885; Apoc. 1895)
RV, mg	Revised Version, margin
SRB	*Scofield Reference Bible* (KJV; 1909)
TCNT	*Twentieth Century New Testament* (1898–1901)
TEV	*Today's English Version* (NT 1966; OT 1976)
TYNDALE	Tyndale New Testament (1524)

WEYMOUTH	*Weymouth's New Testament in Modern Speech* (1903)
WILLIAMS	*New Testament: A Translation in Language of the People* (Williams; 1937)
WYCLIFFE	Wycliffe Bible (1380)
YOUNG	*Literal Translation of the Bible* (Young; 1862)

D. Terms Common to Religious Books

The following abbreviations are recommended for popular and scholarly books. In general, abbreviations for names of organizations and establishments, for some printed references, and for certain technical terms used in scholarly writing are formed without periods. Note, however, that names for denominations are abbreviated with periods, though the periods may be dropped where appropriate.

ab.	abbot *or* abbess
ABA	American Booksellers Association
A.B.Th.	bachelor of arts in theology
ABS	American Bible Society (1816)
A.C.	Anglican church *or* Anglican calendar
ACCC	American Council of Christian Churches (1941)
A.D.	*anno Domini* ("year of our Lord")
AEGM	Anglican Evangelical Group Movement (1906/1923)
Akkad.	Akkadian
A.M.D.G.	*ad maiorem Dei gloriam* ("to the greater glory of God"), motto of the Jesuits
A.M.E.	African Methodist Episcopal
anc.	ancient
Angl.	Anglican
ap.	apostle
abp.	archbishop
Apoc.	Apocalypse
Apocr.	Apocrypha or Apocryphal
APUC	Association for the Promotion of the Unity of Christendom (1857)

Aq.	Aquila's Greek translation of OT
Arab.	Arabic
Aram.	Aramaic
Assyr.	Assyrian
b.	bar/ben (Aram./Heb. for "son of")
Bab.	Babylonian
Bapt.	Baptist
B.C.	before Christ
bl.	blessed
B.C.L.	bachelor of canon law
BCMS	Bible Churchmen's Missionary Society (1922)
B.C.P.	Book of Common Prayer
B.D.	bachelor of divinity
BFBS	British and Foreign Bible Society (1804)
B.H.L.	bachelor of Hebrew letters
bib.	biblical
BM	British Museum
bp.	bishop
B.R.E.	bachelor of religious education
B.S.L.	bachelor of sacred literature
B.V.M.	Blessed Virgin Mary
Can.	Canaanite
card.	cardinal
CBA	Christian Booksellers Association
CCCS	Colonial and Continental Church Society (1838)
CCD	Confraternity of Christian Doctrine
CEF	Child Evangelism Fellowship (1937)
CIM	China Inland Mission (1865)
CLS	Christian Literature Society
cod., codd.	codex, codices
comm(s).	commentary (commentaries)
C.M.	common meter 86.86 (hymnody)
C.M.D.	common meter doubled 86.86 86.86 (hymnody)
C.M.E.	Christian Methodist Episcopal Church
CMS	Church Missionary Society (1799)
CPAS	Church Pastoral Aid Society (1836)
C.R.C.	Christian Reformed Church
C.R.L.	Canons Regular of the Lateran
C.S.	Christian Science

C.S.B.	bachelor of Christian science
C.S.D.	doctor of Christian science
CYO	Catholic Youth Organization
D	Deuteronomist
D.B.	bachelor of divinity
D.C.L.	doctor of canon law
D.D.	doctor of divinity
D.G.	*Deo gratia* ("by the grace of God")
D.H.L.	doctor of Hebrew letters
doct.	doctrine
D.O.M.	*Deo optimo maximo* ("God, the best and greatest")
D.P.	domestic prelate
D.R.E.	doctor of religious education
DSS	Dead Sea Scrolls
D.S.T.	doctor of sacred theology
D.Th. (or D.T.)	doctor of theology
D.V.	*Deo volente* ("God willing")
E	Elohist
E.C.	Eastern calendar
eccl.	ecclesiastic or ecclesiastical
ECPA	Evangelical Christian Publishers Association
Egyp.	Egyptian
E.O.	Eastern Orthodox
ep(p).	epistle(s)
Episc.	Episcopal, Episcopalian
E.T.	English translation
Eth.	Ethiopic
FCA	Fellowship of Christian Athletes (1954)
FOCUS	Fellowship of Christians in Universities and Schools (1961)
G.A.R.B.C.	General Association of Regular Baptist Churches
Gk.	Greek
H	Law of Holiness
H.C.	Holy Communion
Heb.	Hebrew

Hel.	Hellenistic
Hex.	Hexateuch
Hitt.	Hittite
IBS	International Bible Society
ICCU	Intercollegiate Christian Union (1877; later IVF)
ICF	Industrial Christian Fellowship (1918)
IHS	monogram for Greek name for Jesus
IMC	International Missionary Council (1921)
INRI	*Iesus Nazarenus Rex Iudaeorum* ("Jesus of Nazareth, King of the Jews")
IVCF	InterVarsity Christian Fellowship (U.S.; 1939)
IVF	Inter-Varsity Fellowship (Great Britain; 1927)
J	Yahwist (source of Pentateuch)
J"	Jehovah
J.B.C.	bachelor of canon law
J.C.D.	doctor of canon law
Jeh.	Jehovah (Yahweh)
Jerus.	Jerusalem
J T	Jerusalem Talmud
Jud.	Judaism
Lat.	Latin
lex.	lexicon
L.D.S.	Latter-Day Saints
L.L.	Late Latin
L.M.	long meter—88.88 (hymnody)
L.M.D.	long meter doubled 88.88 88.88 (hymnody)
LMS	London Missionary Society (1795)
Luth.	Lutheran
LXX	Septuagint
m or mg	marginal notes in Scripture version
m(m).	martyr(s)
M.Div.	master of divinity
M.E.C.	Methodist Episcopal Church
Meth.	Methodist
mk.	monk
M.L.	Medieval Latin
M.R.E.	master of religious education

MS, MSS	manuscript, manuscripts
MT	Masoretic Text
M.T.S.	master of theological studies
NAE	National Association of Evangelicals
NCC	National Council of Churches
NCCJ	National Conference of Christians and Jews
NEC	National Ecumenical Coalition (1976)
NRB	National Religious Broadcasters
NS	New Series
NT	New Testament
O.C.	Cistercian Order
O.Cart.	Carthusian Order
O.F.M.	Order of Friars Minor (Franciscans)
O.P.	Order of Preachers (Dominicans)
O.S.	Old Syriac
O.S.B.	Order of St. Benedict
O.S.D.	Order of St. Dominic
O.S.M.	Order of the Servants of Mary
OT	Old Testament
P	Priestly Narrative (source of Pentateuch)
Pal.	Palestine
par.	parallel
Patr.	Patriarch
P.C.	Priestly Code
P.C.A.	Presbyterian Church in America
P.C.U.S.A.	Presbyterian Church (U.S.A.)
Pent.	Pentateuch
Pesh.	Peshitta
P.G.	preacher general
Phoen.	Phoenician
pr.	priest
pr. bk.	prayer book
Presb.	Presbyterian
Prot.	Protestant
pseudep.	pseudepigrapha or pseudepigraphal
Q	Quelle (supposed source of Synoptic Gospels)

R.	with refrain (hymnody)
r.	rabbi
rab.	rabbinic
R.C.	Roman Catholic *or* Roman calendar
R.C.C.	Roman Catholic Church
relig.	religion
Rev.	Reverend
Rom.	Roman
Rt. Rev.	Right Reverend
S.A.	Salvation Army (1865)
Sam.	Samaritan
SCLC	Southern Christian Leadership Conference
SCM	Student Christian Movement (1895)
Script.	Scripture
S.D.A.	Seventh-day Adventist
Sem.	Semitic
S.J.	Society of Jesus (Jesuits)
S.M.	short meter — 66.86 (hymnody)
S.M.D.	short meter doubled 66.86 66.86 (hymnody)
SPCK	Society for Promoting Christian Knowledge (1698)
SPG	Society for the Propagation of the Gospel (1701)
Sr.	Sister (of a religious order)
S.S.L.	licentiate in sacred Scripture
St., Sts.	saint, saints
Sta.	saint (female; Italian)
S.T.B.	bachelor of sacred theology
S.T.D.	doctor of sacred theology
Ste.	saint (female; French)
S.T.L.	licentiate of sacred theology
S.T.M.	master of sacred theology
SVM	Student Volunteer Movement (1888)
Symm.	Symmachus's Greek translation of OT
Syr.	Syriac
Talm.	Talmud
Tan.	Tanach (Hebrew Scriptures)
Targ.	Targum
Th.D.	doctor of theology
Theod.	Theodotion's Greek translation of OT
Th.M.	master of theology

theol.	theology, theological
tr.	translation or translated
TR	Textus Receptus
U.I.O.D.G.	*ut in omnibus Deus glorificetur* ("that God may be glorified in all things"), motto of the Benedictine order
UMCA	Universities Mission to Central Africa (1857)
v(v).	verse(s)
Ven.	Venerable
Vulg.	Vulgate (Jerome's Latin Bible).
WCC	World Council of Churches (1948)
WCTU	Women's Christian Temperance Union (1874)
YFC	Youth for Christ (1944)
YMCA	Young Men's Christian Association (1844)
YWCA	Young Women's Christian Association (1855)

VII.
NOTES, REFERENCES, INDEXES

A. Notes

1. Textual annotations are of two general types. *Narrative notes* are used for any comments that could not be appropriately incorporated into the text itself. They can define words or points, comment on the text, provide explanations or expansions, refer the reader to other parts of the text, or provide information peripheral to the text.

   1. Such was Jeremy Taylor's reputation that he was later referred to as the "Shakespeare of divines."
   2. *Euphuistic* is used here to refer specifically to the ornate style of Elizabethan prose.

   Source notes (also called *bibliographic notes*) inform the reader of the sources of quotations and other borrowed information; they can also refer the reader to works that might be of related interest. These two types of notes are not exclusive, however, for a single note can serve as both a narrative note and a source note.

   [3] A. C. Cawley, ed., *Everyman and Medieval Miracle Plays* (New York: Dutton, 1959), 79–108.
   [4] See also Leland Ryken, *Triumphs of the Imagination* (Downers Grove: InterVarsity Press, 1979); and Walter Kaufmann, ed., *Religion from Tolstoy to Camus* (New York: Harper & Row, 1961).

[5] In many of his books Martin E. Marty attempts to get an overview of these tensions in the modern church. Perhaps the most representative of his works to date is Martin E. Marty, *Modern American Religion* (Chicago: Univ. of Chicago Press, 1986).

2. Notes are cited by superscript numbers in the text next to the sentence or word to which the note refers. Where possible, the superscript number should be placed at the end of a sentence so as not to disrupt the reader's attention in the middle of the sentence. While reference numbers in the text are always set in superscript numerals, the corresponding numerals attached to the note may be set in either superscript with no period or in regular type followed by a period. (Examples of both kinds are found in this section.) Symbol reference marks may be preferred to numerals in some cases (see rule 9 in this section).

3. Authors of popular books are encouraged to keep the number of narrative notes to a minimum since annotations intrude upon the reader's attention. In scholarly works narrative notes are often essential to clarify important and complex information, although when possible, the author should still try to keep the number of notes to a minimum. Source notes, of course, must be used in both kinds of books whenever quotations or other information has been borrowed from another source.

4. Notes commonly appear in one of three places: (1) as footnotes at the bottom of the text pages, (2) listed as chapter endnotes at the back of each chapter, or (3) as endnotes at the back of the book.

5. Whether the notes appear as footnotes, endnotes, or chapter endnotes, superscript citations in the text should begin over again at *1* in every new chapter. Superscript numbers should follow all punctuation marks except a dash and should be placed at the end of a sentence or a clause whenever possible. They should be placed at the

end of a block quotation, not with the statement that introduces the block quotation.

6. In the endnotes section in the back matter of a book, the number and title of each chapter should appear as a heading for notes from that chapter so that those notes will be easier to locate.

7. Superscript citation numbers should not be used in a line of display type or after a subheading. If a note applies to an entire chapter, it should be unnumbered and appear on the first page of the chapter as a footnote.

8. Although some writers think footnotes seem more scholarly than endnotes, many publishers are now discouraging the use of footnotes altogether for three reasons: (1) footnotes often unnecessarily distract the reader from the main argument of the book, (2) the small type and narrow leading are often unattractive, and (3) for many photocomposition systems, corrections in footnotes can be far more costly than corrections in endnotes or chapter endnotes. Endnotes, it may be argued, are more of a distraction in that they force the reader to turn to the back of the book each time a superscript citation appears. But ideally, endnotes should be less distracting, for the reader can simply look up those notes that are of special interest.

9. In some cases, footnotes and endnotes might both be used in the same book. If the narrative notes are so closely related to the text that it is not appropriate to set them as endnotes, they should be set as footnotes. In such cases, the footnotes should be cited in the text by symbol reference marks (*, †, ‡, and so on). The endnotes are cited by superscript citation numbers. In books with few narrative footnotes, symbol reference marks should be used instead of superscript numbers. Symbol reference marks are used in the following sequence only if more than one note appears on a particular page. Otherwise, the sequence begins with the asterisk on each new page.

* asterisk or star	¶ paragraph mark
† dagger	then the same marks
‡ double dagger	doubled: **, ††, ‡‡, §§, ¶¶
§ section mark	

10. Titles and degrees are not given with author's names in source notes and should be included in narrative notes only if that information is pertinent.

11. The following information should normally be included, as appropriate, in a source note that cites a book as the source:

Full name of author(s) or editor(s)
Title and subtitle of book
Full name of editor(s) or translator(s), if any
Name of series, and volume and number in the series
Edition, if other than the first
Number of volumes
Facts of publication: city (and state if city is not well known), publisher, and year of publication (all in parentheses)
Volume number
Page number(s) of the citation

6. Winthrop S. Hudson, *Religion in America,* 2d ed. (New York: Charles Scribner's Sons, 1973), 154.

7. John Calvin, *Institutes of the Christian Religion,* ed. John T. McNeill, 2 vols. (Philadelphia: Westminster, 1960), 2:1016.

8. Ruth A. Tucker and Walter Liefeld, *Daughters of the Church* (Grand Rapids: Zondervan, 1987), 100–102.

12. For well-known cities, state names need not be used in notes or bibliographies. The chart of short-form publisher names on pages 133–34 suggests a few cities that are familiar enough to warrant dropping a state name in references. When in doubt, use the state name.

13. A shortened form for listing the publisher's name should be used (see section C of this chapter). Delete such words as *Publisher, Inc., Co., Press,* and *Books.* The words *Press* and *Books* should be retained, however, when a publisher's name might be confused with its parent organiza-

tion or another institution; for instance, the university presses or such publishers as Moody Press or InterVarsity Press. Also, for university presses, it is best to use the longer form, although the article *the* should be dropped and the word *University* may be shortened to *Univ.* Thus, *the University of Chicago Press* could be rendered *Univ. of Chicago Press.*

14. References to classical and some scholarly works appearing in many editions may be designated by division numbers rather than page numbers. This enables citations to be located regardless of the particular edition an author uses. Different levels of division (such as book, section, paragraph, line) are indicated by numerals separated by periods. Commas, en dashes, and semicolons are used for multiple references just as they are in citing page numbers. The numerals are usually Arabic. Using division numbers eliminates the need for volume and page numbers, but notes may contain both forms of notation if desired.

[9]St. Augustine, *Confessions* 9.23–31. [Book 9, sections 23 through 31]

[10]Eusebius, *The History of the Church* 1.2.15, 18. [Book 1, section 2, paragraphs 15 and 18]

[11]William Langland, *Piers Plowman* 5.136–189; 15.1–49. [Canto 5, lines 136 through 189; and canto 15, lines 1 through 49]

[12]John Calvin, *Institutes of the Christian Religion,* ed. John T. McNeill, 4.1.5. [Book 4, chapter 1, paragraph 5. This is the same reference as note 7 in rule number 11 in this section.]

[13]*The Didache,* 2.9.1 [Part 2, section 9, line 1]

15. The following information should normally be included in giving an article from a periodical as the source:

Full name of author(s)
Title
Name of periodical
Volume and issue numbers
Date (in parentheses)
Page number(s)

Note that not all this information is available for every periodical. Popular newspapers and magazines often do not carry volume and issue numbers, and many articles do not carry a by-line. In such cases, as much of the above information as possible should be provided.

14. James Johnson, "Charles G. Finney and a Theology of Revivalism," *Church History* 38 (September 1969): 357.
15. John H. Timmerman, "The Ugly in Art," *Christian Scholar's Review* 7, no. 2–3 (1977): 139.
16. Tom Carson, "Baring the Celtic Soul of U2," *Los Angeles Times Book Review* (March 27, 1988), 15.
17. "Bruce Cockburn: Singer in a Dangerous Time," *Sojourners* 17, no. 1 (January 1988): 28–35.

16. For both book and periodical references, "Ibid." takes the place of the author's name, the title, and page number when all of that information is identical to the information in the immediately preceding note. If the author and title are the same but the page reference has changed, then "Ibid." may be used with the new page reference. For books intended for a general or popular readership, authors are encouraged to use repeated short-form references instead of "Ibid." (See next paragraph for the proper elements of a short-form reference.) "Ibid." is most appropriately used in academic and scholarly books that contain a large number of citations.

[18]Nicholas Wolterstorff, *Art in Action* (Grand Rapids: Eerdmans, 1980), 45.
[19]Ibid., 47.
[20]Ibid.

17. When a second reference occurs later than immediately following the first reference (in which case "Ibid." would not apply), a short-form reference should be used in both scholarly and popular works. This is preferred over the older system of using "op. cit." or "loc. cit." A short-form reference should include the author's last name, a shortened form of the title (if it is more than five words)

sufficient to identify the book cited previously in a full note, and a page reference.

21. James Samuel Preus, *From Shadow to Promise: Old Testament Interpretation from Augustine to Young Luther* (Cambridge, Mass.: Belknap, 1969), 50.
22. Wolterstorff, Nicholas, *Art in Action*, 97.
23. Preus, *From Shadow to Promise*, 58.

18. Whenever possible, exact page references should be given in lieu of using a single page number followed by *ff.* Such abbreviations as *vol.* and *p.* or *pp.* are unnecessary unless their omission will result in ambiguity.

19. Abbreviations of states in notes or bibliographies should be given in conventional form with a period. Two-letter postal forms should be reserved for actual mailing addresses. (See chart on pages 108–10.)

B. Bibliographies

1. A bibliography lists significant works related to the topic of the book, to points discussed in the book, or to works on related topics. Its purpose is to inform the reader of other works that might be of interest. In most cases, a bibliography should not include the titles of works that were merely quoted, referred to, or important in the research of the volume unless those works are also related to the topic of the book.

2. In a bibliography authors, editors, translators, or compilers of works are listed last name first, and the list is compiled alphabetically. No titles or degrees are used with names. When two or more names are given for a single entry, the first is listed last-name-first; a comma follows that name, and the other names are listed first-name-first. If the bibliography is broken down under subheads, then each section is alphabetized separately.

3. The following information should normally be included, where appropriate, in a bibliographical entry for a book:

Full name of author(s) or editor(s)
Complete title of book (and complete subtitle, if any)
Full name of editor(s) or translator(s), if any
Name of series, and volume and number in the series
Edition, if other than the first
Number of volumes
City where book was published (and state if city is not well known)
Name of publisher
Year of publication

De Gasztold, Carmen Bernos. *Prayers from the Ark.* Translated by
    Rumer Godden. New York: Viking, 1947.
Johnson, James Weldon. *God's Trombones.* New York: Viking,
    1927.
Tennyson, G. B. and Edward E. Ericson, Jr., eds. *Religion and
    Modern Literature: Essays in Theory and Criticism.* Grand
    Rapids: Eerdmans, 1975.

As with notes, a shortened form for listing the publisher's name should be used.

4. The following information should normally be included
    in a bibliographical entry for an article from a periodical:

Full name of author(s) or editor(s)
Complete title of article (and complete subtitle if any)
Name of periodical
Volume number (and issue number if any)
Date (in parentheses)
Page number(s) of article

As with source notes, not all this information is available
for every periodical. In such cases, as much of the
information as possible should be provided.

Aeschliman, M. D. "Flickering Candles in the Winds of Woe."
    Books & Religion 15, no. 6 (Winter 1988): 3, 29.
"Fighting Isms and Schisms." *Christian History* 4, no. 3 (1987): 29.
Ubell, Earl. "Surgeon General C. Everett Koop Has an Idea: A
    Battle Plan to Save Your Life." *Parade* (April 10, 1988), 16–17.

5. A less formal type of bibliography—a "For Further
    Reading" list—may be more appropriate than a thorough

bibliography in some books. Such lists should follow the format of the formal bibliography but might conceivably contain only author and title.

Boyer, Robert H., and Kenneth J. Zahorski. *Vision of Wonder: An Anthology of Christian Fantasy.*
Chesterton, G. K. *The Man Who Was Thursday.*
L'Engle, Madeleine. *A Wrinkle in Time.*
MacDonald, George. *The Princess and the Goblin.*

C. Selected Religious Publishers in Short Form

The following list is provided as a quick reference for correct spelling and shortened form of some well-known religious publishers. Note that some cities are well-known enough to warrant the omission of state names.

Publisher	Location	Short-Form Name
Abbey Press	St. Meinrad, Ind.	Abbey
Abingdon Press	Nashville	Abingdon
Accent Books	Denver	Accent
Antioch Publishing Co.	Yellow Springs, Ohio	Antioch
Augsburg Publishing House	Minneapolis	Augsburg
Ave Maria Press	Notre Dame, Ind.	Ave Maria
Back to the Bible	Lincoln, Neb.	Back to the Bible
Baker Book House	Grand Rapids	Baker
Ballantine/Epiphany	New York	Ballantine/Epiphany
Banner of Truth	Carlisle, Pa.	Banner of Truth
Baptist Publishing House	Texarkana, Tex.	Baptist
Bethany House Publishers	Minneapolis	Bethany House
Broadman Press	Nashville	Broadman
Collier Books/Macmillan	New York	Collier/Macmillan
Concordia Publishing House	St. Louis	Concordia
David C. Cook Publishing Co.	Elgin, Ill.	David C. Cook

Cowley Publications	Cambridge, Mass.	Cowley
Creation House	Altamonte, Fla.	Creation House
Crossway Books	Westchester, Ill.	Crossway
Doubleday Co.	Garden City	Doubleday
Wm. B. Eerdmans Publishing Co.	Grand Rapids	Eerdmans
Fortress Press	Philadelphia	Fortress
Harper & Row, Publishers	San Francisco	Harper & Row
Harvest House	Eugene, Ore.	Harvest House
Herald Press	Scottdale, Pa.	Herald
Ignatius Press	Harrison, N.Y.	Ignatius
InterVarsity Press	Downers Grove, Ill.	InterVarsity Press
John Knox Press	Atlanta	John Knox
Kregel Publications	Grand Rapids	Kregel
The Macmillan Co.	New York	Macmillan
Moody Press	Chicago	Moody Press
Mott Media	Milford, Mich.	Mott Media
Multnomah Press	Portland, Ore.	Multnomah Press
NavPress	Colorado Springs	NavPress
Thomas Nelson, Inc.	Nashville	Nelson
Paulist Press	Mahwah, N.J.	Paulist
Regal Books	Ventura, Calif.	Regal
Fleming H. Revell Co.	Old Tappan, N.J.	Revell
Servant Publications	Ann Arbor, Mich.	Servant
Harold Shaw Publishers	Wheaton, Ill.	Harold Shaw
Tyndale House Publishers Inc.	Wheaton, Ill.	Tyndale House
Victor Books	Wheaton, Ill.	Victor
The Westminster Press	Philadelphia	Westminster
Word, Inc.	Waco, Tex.	Word
Zondervan Publishing House	Grand Rapids	Zondervan

D. Scripture References

Rules for Scripture references are scattered through various sections of this manual but are reiterated here for easy reference.

1. Authors should inform readers of which Scripture version they use predominantly. This notice may be given in the introduction, the preface, or any other place where it is not likely to be overlooked. Since in many cases extensive use of modern translations requires a permission notice and credit line, the copyright page is often the most convenient place for stating the Scripture version. The following form is acceptable, although the granting copyright holder may prefer a different form, in which case that form should be strictly adhered to.

> Unless otherwise noted, all Scripture references in this book are taken from the [Version], copyright © [year and copyright holder]. Used by permission of [permission grantor].

2. When a general note regarding a predominant Scripture version has been provided, the author should not indicate the version when references to that version are made in the text. The reader should only be informed when an alternate version is used. This is done by placing the abbreviation of the alternate version next to the Scripture reference. These abbreviations are usually set in small caps without periods. Names of versions that don't lend themselves to abbreviation should also be set in small caps. When used in combination with the Scripture reference itself, these abbreviations should not be preceded by a comma. Abbreviations of Scripture versions may also be used in running text and notes. (A list of abbreviations of the most common Bible versions in English begins on page 115.)

> "Love is patient, love is kind. It does not envy" (1 Cor. 13:4). [No version is cited; the predominant version in this case is the NIV.]
> "Loue is pacient & curteous, loue envyeth not" (1 Cor. 13:4 COVERDALE).
> "Charity suffereth long, and is kind; charity envieth not" (1 Cor. 13:4 KJV).
> The musical qualities of the NIV, COVERDALE, and KJV differ significantly.

3. When an author uses a personal translation or para-phrase, this should be indicated in a general note at the beginning of the book (if it is the predominant version) or in a note attached to each specific reference. In the latter case, the phrase *author's translation* or *author's para-phrase* should suffice. Such a phrase, however, is best preceded by a comma.

"Love is content to wait and is considerate. It's not envious" (1 Cor. 13:4, author's paraphrase).

4. A colon separates chapter from verse.

Mark 2:17   1 Peter 3:12

5. A semicolon separates one chapter-and-verse reference from another. If the second chapter-and-verse reference applies to the same book of the Bible, the name of the book should not be repeated.

John 3:3; 10:10; Acts 16:31

6. No space should precede or follow a colon in a Bible reference. There should be space following but not preceding a comma or a semicolon.

7. An en dash is used between consecutive verse numbers. A comma separates nonconsecutive numbers of the same chapter.

John 3:1–6   John 3:15–16   Acts 1:1–8, 13, 16

8. An en dash is also used to indicate several chapters of a Bible book inclusively in a reference or to indicate that a citation begins in one chapter and ends in another.

Gen. 1–11   Gal. 5:26–6:5

9. Books of the Bible should be spelled out, not abbreviated, when the reference appears in running text or when the book alone is referred to. An exception may be made in scholarly or reference works that contain so many references to books of the Bible that abbreviations are needed for the sake of brevity. Also, if many references

appear in parentheses, it is acceptable to abbreviate books of the Bible. Two standard styles of abbreviating books of the Bible are commonly accepted: one for general books and another for scholarly books. A complete list appears on pages 111–15.

10. In references following block quotations of Scripture, the names of Bible books may be spelled out or abbreviated at the author's or editor's discretion, but the same form should be used consistently throughout a manuscript. Either of the following forms may be used:

> No, in all these things we are more than conquerors through him who loved us. For I am convinced that neither death nor life, . . . nor anything else in all creation, will be able to separate us from the love of God that is in Christ Jesus our Lord. (Romans 8:37–39 NIV)

> . . . will be able to separate us from the love of God that is in Christ Jesus our Lord.
> —Romans 8:37–39 NIV

11. The abbreviation for *verse* is *v.*; for *verses*, *vv.*

12. Arabic numerals, not Roman numerals, are used in all parts of Scripture references.

1 Samuel 15:22   2 Corinthians 4

13. It is preferable not to use *a* or *b* with a verse number to indicate that only a portion of a verse is being quoted or referred to. The context usually makes this fact clear. It may be appropriate to use *a* or *b* if the several parts of a verse are being examined successively and the author wishes to indicate one of those parts.

14. For run-in quotes with Scripture references, place the period or other punctuation after the parenthesis containing the reference. If the quotation contains a question mark or exclamation point, place it with the text and place any other needed punctuation after the parenthesis.

"Here is your king" (John 19:14).
"Take him away! Take him away! Crucify him!" (John 19:15).

E. Indexes

1. Although many kinds of indexes exist, they all serve the same function: to make certain portions of the text more accessible to the reader. Not all books need an index. Devotional and inspirational books, for example, usually do not contain the kind of information that makes an index appropriate. But any work presenting facts that might be used for reference or research can benefit from a good index.

   Ordinarily, the author prepares the index as part of his or her responsibility to provide a complete and acceptable manuscript. The author, in fact, is the ideal indexer since no one else has as clear and comprehensive an understanding of the contents of the book. The author may opt to hire a professional or to have the publisher hire a professional to compile the index, the expense in either case being borne by the author. When the publisher hires the indexer, the fee can usually be deducted from the author's royalties.

2. There are two principal types of indexes common to religious publishing: the subject–proper-name index and the Scripture index. The first kind will be dealt with in the following paragraphs. The Scripture index will be described in a paragraph at the end of this section.

   Other kinds of indexes are the title-and-first-line index (for books of hymns and poetry), the concordance (common to Bibles), and the index of place names (common to atlases). An index can be tailored to almost any kind of book in which information needs to be organized for accessibility.

3. In many cases, there may be an advantage to splitting the subject–proper-name index into separate indexes: a subject index and a proper-name index. Indexes are most

commonly set in double columns to conserve space, but specific designs may differ. Two typographical styles exist: the paragraph style and the column style. Paragraph style is convenient when space is a consideration; column style, however, tends to make each entry slightly easier to read. In both styles, commas are used before page numbers. In the paragraph style, a colon separates the main heading from the subentries, while in column style, no additional punctuation is generally used. The following examples illustrate the two styles.

Paragraph Style	Column Style
Heaven: NT conceptions of, 28–32; OT conceptions of, 32–33; pagan views of, 20–25; theological implications of, 33	Heaven, 12–20 NT conceptions of, 28–32 OT conceptions of, 32–33 pagan views of, 20–25 theological implications of, 33
Helen, St. (mother of Constantine): abandonment of, 133; advocacy of Christianity, 160, 167, 180–84; birth of Constantine, 126; her marriage, 120; her restoration under Constantine, 150–52, 160	Helen, St. (mother of Constantine) abandonment of, 133 advocacy of Christianity, 160, 167, 180–84 birth of Constantine, 126 marriage, 120 restoration under Constantine, 150–52, 160

4. This manual recommends the letter-for-letter style of alphabetization for indexes as opposed to word-for-word style. Although neither style is likely to confuse readers, letter-for-letter style is slightly easier to read. Both styles alphabetize as though words with hyphens or apostrophes were set solid, and both alphabetize only those word units that precede any commas. If two words are identical up to the point of the comma, then the information after the comma should be used for the basis of arranging the identical words alphabetically. The two styles may be contrasted by examining the following:

Letter-for-letter	Word-for-Word
Old Believers	Old Believers
Oldcastle, Sir John	Old Catholics
Old Catholics	old covenant
old covenant	Old Latin Versions
Oldham, Joseph	Oldcastle, Sir John
Oldham, Martin	Oldham, Joseph
Oldham Library	Oldham, Martin
Old-Home Week	Oldham Library
Old Latin Versions	Old-Home Week
Olds, Benjamin	Olds, Benjamin

5. Subentries under each index heading may be listed in three ways: (1) alphabetically, which, as the most common and most versatile, is the preferred method for most indexes; (2) chronologically, used mainly for indexes of predominantly biographical information; (3) and numerically by page number, which should be reserved for simple indexes that do not contain a large number of subentries. Only one style should be used throughout an index. If the index is set in paragraph style, a colon separates the entry heading from the subentries, and semicolons separate subentries from each other.

In alphabetizing subentries, articles (such as *the* and *a*) and pronouns (such as *him, her,* and *their*) are generally ignored; that is, the entry is alphabetized according to the key word that occurs after such introductory words.

6. Cross references are an important element of any thorough index. They indicate where alternate entries or additional information might be found under other headings. In a paragraph-style index, a cross reference that includes the whole entry is placed at the end of the entry; in column style, such an inclusive reference is placed after the main-entry heading. In both styles, when only a subentry is being cross referenced, then the cross reference appears immediately after the subentry. The word *see* indicates that an entirely different heading should be referred to, and the words *see also* indicate that

additional information may be found under another entry. The word *see*, whether alone or in the phrase *see also*, is usually capped, set in italics, and preceded by a period. In paragraph style, however, the cross reference is placed in parentheses and the word *see* is lowercased when only the subentry is being cross referenced.

Paragraph Style	Column Style
Bird, William. *See* Byrd, William	Bird, William. *See* Byrd, William
Bishop's Bible, the, 182, 188. *See also* Bibles: before 1611	Bishop's Bible, the, 182, 188. *See also* Bibles: before 1611
Blake, William: paintings of, 228–30; poetry of, 233–39 (*see also* Religious Poetry); his visions, 211. *See also* Artists; Painters	Blake, William. *See also* Artists; Painters. paintings of, 233–39. *See also* Religious Poetry his visions, 211.

7. Scripture indexes inform the reader of all the Scripture quotations used in a book. Most often they only contain references to those Scriptures that are actually quoted, although for some scholarly works the index may also include those Scripture verses that are referred to but not quoted. The Scripture index is usually set in double columns and is arranged in the same order as the books of the Bible itself. Within each book of the Bible, entries are listed numerically by chapter and verse numbers; a chapter-only reference precedes any chapter-and-verse references for that same chapter. The most common form is as follows:

Genesis		Exodus	
1	71	6	27
1–3	113–14	6:14–25	28
1:1	7, 12, 117	15:21	33
1:1–13	7, 18	20:1–17	98, 100–101
1:1–19	189		
2:4–7	60–61		

VIII.
EDITING

A. The Role of the Editor

Editing involves a consideration of many aspects of content, style, and design. Editors have the responsibility to combine these elements into a cohesive whole that gives the best possible expression to an author's ideas, is consistent with the publisher's standards and purpose, and gives the book a pleasing "personality."

Good editing requires that editors visualize at the outset what the finished product should be like and seek to capture that image in word and symbol. There are two functions that are often termed *editing*, though these functions are quite different in intent and responsibility.

1. *Content editing*, or *substantive editing*, concerns the arrangement of the author's ideas in words. Good editing requires changes in words, phrases, sentences, or even long passages to make a book accurate, complete, clear, and precise. Content editors seek to eliminate discrepancies, buttress viewpoints, clarify the obscure, provide missing information, and reorganize material as needed. They work directly with the author in suggesting revisions. Content editing is dynamic. Each book requires individualistic treatment; for this reason many editors

often provide authors with a complete marked-up copy of the edited manuscript or print-out.

The term *style* may refer to literary expression. Literary style is creative, instinctive, and individualistic. The content editor should always allow authors to say what they wish in their own distinctive way; but the editor is also responsible to suggest ways of enhancing that expression by using aesthetic qualities of language. Good literary style is inevitably intertwined with content because the subject matter and author's purposes affect tone, reading level, and degree of formality.

Design is the combination of typographical, spatial, and artistic elements that give a book its physical appearance. It is an integral part of the book's personality. A book's editor and designer are ultimately responsible for its graphic and typographical layout. Generally authors are not involved in the design process.

2. *Copy editing.* In publishing, the term *style* may also refer to a "house style," or press style, which deals with mechanical aspects of language, such as capitalization, spelling, grammar, use of numbers, and punctuation. Making a manuscript conform to house style is the domain of copy editing. This manual attempts to establish a standard of style for religious publishing.

When possible, a copy editor also checks the accuracy of dates, quotations, references, and factual information, although the accuracy of such information is ultimately the author's responsibility. A copy editor's opportunities for making changes in an author's manuscript are restricted to obvious errors, inaccuracies, ambiguities, and inelegancies, and the copy editor's interaction with the author is limited to occasional queries. The copy editor should not presume to make the kinds of dynamic revisions or suggestions that are properly the domain of the author and the content editor.

B. Editing on Paper

1. In editing on paper, clarity is essential. Since a typist will have to prepare the manuscript for typesetting, the editor should make sure that all editorial notations are as clear and as clean as possible. Pencil allows for erasure and is therefore preferred by many editors, but pencil also smudges more easily than pen. Pen, on the other hand, is often cleaner but does not allow for clean corrections.

2. In most cases printing is preferable to handwriting because it will be more legible to the typist.

3. It is advisable for the copy editor to work in a different color pen or pencil than the content editor.

4. For lengthy insertions in a paper manuscript, the new material should be typed on a full-size page and inserted after the page on which the insertion is to be made. Again, the placement of all insertions should be clearly marked. Inserted pages should be given the same number as the page they follow but with the addition of a lowercase *a*, *b*, *c*, and so on.

5. Editorial queries and notes are most conveniently listed on a separate sheet of paper with page and line references. Queries and notes in the margins of the manuscript can easily confuse the typesetter and end up in the proofs. If an occasional short query or note is inserted in margins of the text, the editor should remember the proofreader's rule that anything not meant to be typeset should be circled.

6. On paper, editorial notation uses symbols and markings similar to standard proofreading signs, but with one difference: editorial work is done in the text itself, while proofreading corrections are indicated in the text with a symbol and in the margin with an annotation.

IX.
PROOFREADING

The proofreader is responsible for making sure that typeset material conforms to the editor's wishes in both content and design.

Since the advent of word processing, there can be as many as six proofreading stages in book production: print-out, first proofs, second proofs or repros, page corrections, camera copy, and silverprints. These steps will vary from publisher to publisher; for instance, many publishers proofread first and even second proofs on a word-processing terminal. For those publishers who do follow these six stages, the print-out stage is often skipped. When a print-out is done it is usually checked by the author. First proofs are assigned to a proofreader and are usually checked simultaneously by the author. Second proofs are also assigned to a proofreader. The last three stages are usually checked by the editor in charge of the project.

A. Print-outs

In computerized editing, print-outs are sent to the author at the editor's discretion. This is usually done before first proofs have been run, and this step allows an author a chance to review the book for changes before seeing it in proofs. Often, scheduling does not allow time for a print-out stage, in which case the author will be sent a copy of the first proofs on which to check for errors.

B. First Proofs

Ideally all mistakes should be discovered and corrected by the end of the first-proof stage.

In traditional proofreading, the proofreader checks the proofs (*live copy*) against the manuscript (*dead copy*) to ensure that proof copy corresponds word for word with the edited manuscript. With the advent of word processing, however, it is usually not possible to provide the proofreader with an accurate manuscript against which to check the typeset copy. In this case the proofreader must read the proofs without reference to an authoritative manuscript. This entails checking the accuracy of spelling against the dictionary, and checking for correct style against the publisher's accepted manual of style, and any other references provided by the publisher. The proofreader is responsible to see that all typographical specifications (*specs*) called for by the editor are carried out correctly.

Correcting typographical errors is the proofreader's main objective. These kinds of errors should be marked in first proofs:

Poor spacing (between letters, words, illustrations, lines, and headings)
Wrong alignment or indentations
Incorrect placement, size, or typeface of headings
Wrong typeface or size of text area
Misspellings (refer to *Webster's*)
Footnotes out of order
Incorrect reduction of footnotes or extracts
Poor word divisions
Make-up problems, that is, less than full line on first line of text (*widow*), fewer than two lines below a heading at the bottom of a page, or fewer than four lines on a page ending a chapter.

Every correction on a proof requires two marks; one in the text and one in the margin. A caret or slash is usually used to locate the error in the text; the appropriate proofreader's mark is then made in the margin. Standard symbols are listed on pages 152–53. They may also be found on pages 94–95 of the *Chicago Manual of Style* and on page 943 of *Webster's Ninth New Collegiate Dictionary*. Proofreaders should flag any cross references within the book so they can be filled in on final pages. They should also flag places where artwork (illustrations, charts, figures, and so on) will be needed.

The proofreader should use black pen and initial each proof page. This will certify that the proofreading is complete.

Ascertaining the style of each project and being consistent within that style are an important part of the proofreader's job, because not all projects will conform to the most recognized or standard usage. Proofreaders are encouraged to prepare a style sheet for themselves to enforce conformity within individual projects, noting special terminology, troublesome spellings, and typographical specifications. For complex projects the editor should provide a style sheet for the proofreader.

Proofreaders are limited in their right to make editorial changes, but are encouraged to query the editor if a passage seems unclear in content or grammatical form or if factual information seems false. Proofreaders query the editor by placing a question mark to the far right of the margin noting the problem or suggested correction. Queries are concise and circled, and the page on which they occur should be marked with a paper clip. When the proofreader has a query, he or she should call the editor's attention to it by writing on the page in a different color pen. Marking queries in a different color ink is preferable to affixing tags to the page, since tags can easily become separated from the pages. If a query involves more than this type of short note, proofreaders can prepare a query sheet indicating the page and line on which their question occurs, to avoid cluttering the proofs.

C. Second Proofs

At the second-proof stage the proofreader sees that each correction called for on first proofs has been made properly; if it has, it should be checked off. Usually the proofreader will be provided with both the first proofs and the author's corrections.

After checking that all corrections have been made, the proofreader reads through the entire project, marking any errors overlooked on first proofs and checking for sense, proper arrangement of material, and new incorrect hyphenations. The proofreader does not read line for line against the first proofs or the author's copy but may refer to either. Any added material that has had no previous reading must be carefully scrutinized.

Second proofs normally constitute completed pages with folios and running heads: these are checked for proper sequence, position, and typeface. The order and numbering of footnotes, both in the text and in the list of notes, is double-checked at this stage. The proofreader also makes sure all chapter titles and running heads are consistent with the titles given in the table of contents, and then inserts correct page numbers into the table of contents. Cross references in the text are also filled in by locating the page reference in the manuscript and noting the material referred to, and then finding this material and its final page number in the second proofs. The proofreader spot-checks page lengths and scrutinizes overall appearance, especially noting consistency in spacing. Queries should be few at this stage.

D. Page Corrections

When a correction is called for on second proofs, only the affected pages are reset. These corrected pages are usually proofread by the editor, who checks to see that the corrections have been properly made. This involves looking up the page in the second proofs on which each correction is called for and scanning the material around the correction to ensure that no additional errors have been introduced. These corrected pages are then inserted into the final proofs by the typesetter.

E. Camera Copy

Camera copy provides the last opportunity to correct mistakes before negatives are made. Overall page appearance is the main concern at this stage. The editor checks that all page corrections have been done correctly. The running heads and folios are examined for order and placement and are compared with the table of contents for consistency. Copyright information is double-checked. Chapter titles and artwork that have been pasted in are checked for proper placement and general appearance. The length of facing pages is closely examined. Many times the editor reads the bottom line of a page and the top line of the following page to ensure correct order of copy.

F. Silverprints

Silverprints, also called blueprints or "blues," are contact prints made from negatives by the printer. These prints are checked by the editor for general appearance. After the editor makes sure that everything is in order, that all corrections have been made, the book is ready for the press. No changes can be made after the editor has approved silverprints, because the next step is platemaking for the printing press.

Black spots and spots in letters caused by faulty negatives are circled for removal. Signature marks, located on the spine of each signature and used for collating the book, are checked for proper placement. Also, the pages should be checked at this stage to make sure that they are in the correct numerical sequence.

Problems that may not show clearly on camera-ready copy are often easily spotted in silverprints. For instance, inconsistency in space between a pasted-up line and adjacent lines, space between running head and text, or straightness of pasted-in material are problems often not found until the silverprint stage. But changes on silverprints are costly and involve shooting new negatives. In fact, corrections become more troublesome and expensive to make with each successive stage of production; so it is important to examine proofs and materials carefully each time a project comes into the hands of an editor or proofreader. When corrections do need to be made on silverprints, the editor should mark the problem clearly and attach a paperclip to the page so that the long side of the paperclip extends onto the page of the correction.

G. Miscellaneous

Certain typefaces have idiosyncracies that the proofreader and
editor should be aware of. For instance, some Souvenir types
run *r* and *n* so closely together they may appear as an *m*.
Baskerville and Bembo types usually seem smaller when compared with other faces in the same point size. Melior's ligatures
don't always run together. In many typefaces an *f* followed by a
quotation mark or question mark will require a hair space (hr#)
inserted between them, as will some opening parentheses
followed by a capital *J*.

H. Standard Proofreading Symbols

Insert Copy

e	Insert lettr.	C/J	[Insert brackets.]
word	Insert a.	•••	Insert ellipsis.
See p.x	Insert new copy.	⸸/⸸	Insert quotation marks.
⌢g	Insert endin letter.	slash	Insert solidus slash.
b⌣	Insert eginning letter.		Insert apostrophe
#	Insert space.	⸰	[Buechners]
⊙	Insert period.	accent	Insert accent. [cliche]
↑	Insert comma.	set ?	Insert question mark.
;/	Insert semicolon;/	set !	Insert exclamation point.
⊙	Insert colon.	⸰	Insert superior number.
⸗/	Insert hyphen. [born again]		

⊥m	Insert em dash or long dash.
⊥N	Insert en dash. [1898 1963]
(/)	(Insert parentheses.)

Delete Copy

℘	Delete character.
℘	Delete and close up.
℘	Delete word word.
℘	Delete line.

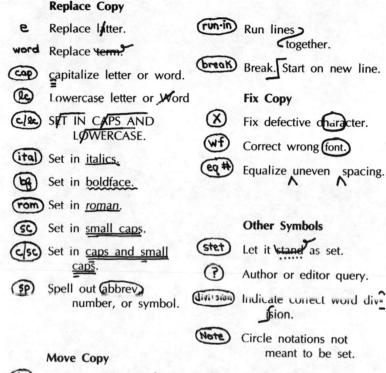

Replace Copy

e   Replace letter.

word   Replace ~~term.~~

(cap)   capitalize letter or word.

(lc)   Lowercase letter or Word

(c/lc)   SET IN CAPS AND LOWERCASE.

(ital)   Set in _italics._

(bf)   Set in **boldface.**

(rom)   Set in _roman_.

(sc)   Set in small caps.

(c/sc)   Set in caps and small caps.

(sp)   Spell out (abbrev.) number, or symbol.

Move Copy

(tr)   Transpose characters.

(tr)   words Transpose.

☐   ☐ Indent one em space.

⊏   ⊏ Move left.

⊐   Move right.

⊐⊏   Center. ⊏

(align)   ‖ Align copy.

◡   Close space.

(less #)   Less ⋀ space.

¶   ¶ Start new paragraph.

(run-in)   Run lines together.

(break)   Break. Start on new line.

Fix Copy

(X)   Fix defective character.

(wf)   Correct wrong (font.)

(eq #)   Equalize uneven spacing.

Other Symbols

(stet)   Let it stand as set.

(?)   Author or editor query.

(division)   Indicate correct word division.

(Note)   Circle notations not meant to be set.

/   **Slashes are used to:**

r/lc/   Separate corections in a single line.

e ‖‖   Rpeat sam corrction in a single line.

X.
COMPUTERS AND
BOOKS

Back when books were typeset, printed, and bound by hand, it could take as long as a year to produce a single edition. With the advent of word processing, phototypesetting, and high-speed printing and binding—it can still take a year! Although technology has streamlined almost every aspect of bookmaking, one fact remains: a book is still a product of the human mind. Only people can write, edit, and check books for accuracy.

In the publishing house as in the world at large, technological innovation has had the annoying habit of creating one new problem for every two old ones it solves. Since the value of computerization must be measured in terms of increased efficiency, any new automated procedure that results in less efficiency must be reexamined. This chapter looks at some of the innovations that affect the author, the publisher, and the proofreader. It defines some problems and offers a few solutions.

A. The Writer's Word Processor

Most writers approach the word processor as a kind of glorified typewriter. While surpassing even the electronic typewriter as a labor-saving device, the word processor, like its predecessor, is used largely to generate a paper copy of a manuscript, and for these writers, computerization has refined, rather than redirected the traditional process of bookmaking. Other writers have begun to submit copies of their floppy disks to their publishers in lieu of paper manuscripts, an increasingly common procedure that saves the publisher the time and cost of having to retype (*rekeyboard*) the manuscript onto their own word processors and typesetting machines. As will be explained later, this has revolutionized certain facets of publishing. For both kinds of writers, however, word processing has introduced some problems.

Vulnerability. Chief among these problems is damaged disks. The magnetic, or floppy, disks used in most word processors are susceptible to the same hazards as any paper manuscript, but they are also vulnerable to a host of other dangers that can result in negating the labor-saving benefits of computerization. This is also true of the magnetic and paper tapes common to some older systems.

Manuscripts have always been vulnerable, of course. Most writers can tell horror stories of unique copies of yet-to-be-printed books that were left on a bus or accidentally burned in a fire. Word processing has the added potential of actually destroying an author's work almost as it is being created. Word-processor users have their own horror stories. The information stored on a floppy disk can be accidentally erased, garbled by electrical surges, and rendered irretrievable in hundreds of fiendishly unexpected ways.

To minimize such problems, the author should:

1. Be thoroughly familiar with the word processor's operating manual. The author should know how to copy disks, determine available disk space, and perform smoothly all other functions intended to minimize damage.

2. Make sure that the word processor is regularly cleaned according to the manufacturer's instructions.

3. Always work on relatively fresh disks. Although tales abound of five-year-old floppy disks that are still functioning like new, most manufacturers will not guarantee the reliability of their disks for more than a year. After that, the risk of losing data increases.

4. Store the disks carefully. Keep them well away from dust, moisture, extreme temperatures, pets, and magnetic fields (such as radios, stereo speakers, the computer itself, or even magnetic clasps on cabinet doors). Paper clips that have been stored in a magnetic holder can retain enough magnetism to garble an entire sector of a floppy disk. Writing on disks with ball-point pens can also cause damage. These and other dangers are listed on most disk-storage envelopes.

5. Keep at least one disk copy (a *back-up*) of each computer document every time that document is revised.

6. Print out at least one paper copy (called a *hard copy*) of each phase of writing or revision as soon as possible.

Although these few commonsense rules will not prevent the loss of a floppy disk on a bus or in a fire, they will help minimize the possibility of losing hours of effort in one irrecoverable instant

Multiple copies. Another problem that writers face can be summed up in the question: Where does the book really exist? Whether the book is submitted on paper, on disk, or both, the author and the publisher should specify at every stage of editing and revision who has the authoritative copy.

An example: An author submits to a publisher a paper copy of a manuscript that was generated by the author's word processor. The publisher hires a typist to type the manuscript onto the publisher's word processor for editing and phototypeset-ting. While the editor is editing the book on the publisher's word processor, however, the author decides to revise the manuscript by rewriting several chapters on his or her word processor, after which the author sends a new print-out of the manuscript to the publisher. The editor then faces this problem: two different copies of the same book now exist—an edited copy on the publisher's word processor and a revised paper copy from the author. Integrating these two copies can be an expensive process, requiring each of the author's changes to be checked word-for-word against the publisher's computer copy. In a sense, it adds a proofreading stage even before the book has gone to proofs. Once again the benefit of computerization has been lost.

The author and the editor should agree on where and when revisions and corrections should be made. After submitting the paper manuscript, the author should limit revisions only to print-outs or proofs provided by the publisher, or else the author should clearly highlight exactly those changes that were made. In the case of floppy-disk submissions, the author and editor can send a disk copy of the book back and forth for editing, revision, and reediting as long as it is clear who has the definitive, workable copy at any given stage.

Compatibility and format. One of the revolutionary changes brought about by the computerization of publishing is that, for the author who submits a manuscript to the publisher on floppy disk, the author in effect becomes the typesetter. The publisher can use the author's keystrokes recorded on a floppy disk as the basis for the typeset proofs, and this has forced editors and authors alike to rethink traditional bookmaking. It is now possible, for example, to write, edit, revise, proofread, and typeset a book entirely on computers so that no paper needs to be used before the book is in print. In the future, printing on paper might even be eliminated in favor of simply reproducing computer copies of the book on floppy disk for people to read on their home computers.

In this chapter it is impossible to adequately convey the many format problems that submitting "electronic manuscripts" entails; but in most cases, the publisher should provide the author with guidelines that address such questions as software, preferred formats, special characters, and simple typesetting codes. Compatibility of software is not the least of these considerations. The author and publisher need to work together so that the author can prepare the manuscript in a way that will facilitate its eventual typesetting.

In traditional typing, a manuscript is customarily made to look as much like a finished book as possible, a habit that has unfortunately been carried over into word processing. This includes the typing of titles in capital letters, adding extra returns between heads and text, indenting block quotations several spaces from each margin. Some word processors can even enlarge and reduce type sizes and indicate several different fonts.

The author who plans to submit a manuscript on floppy disk to a publisher, however, needs to think in an entirely new way. The priority should be to present as simple and as consistent a manuscript as possible, one that will allow the publisher's computer to most easily adapt the raw keystrokes to a usable form for typesetting. All type sizes, line spaces, font changes, etc., that are to appear in the printed book will be made by special codes, not by special formats that may be specific only to the author's word processor.

Since authors are in effect providing the keystrokes that will be transformed into typeset copy, they should understand a few basic differences between word processing and typesetting. The following suggestions may even be helpful to the author who is submitting a paper print-out to a publisher if that publisher is planning to have the manuscript scanned and entered into a computer by electronic means. Although not complete, the following list suggests a few items the author should be aware of:

1. Ideally the author should use no graphic symbols except the return symbol at the ends of paragraphs. Tabs, indents, and other formatting commands will only have to be eliminated before most typesetting systems can use the keystrokes. Double returns should be used between paragraphs. The publisher should provide the author with a list of basic typesetting codes to be used in place of the word processor's graphic symbols to distinguish paragraphs, extracts, heads, and other common elements of a manuscript.

2. In general the author should strive to prepare as clean and as uncluttered a disk manuscript as possible. This means avoiding the use of many other special format features that may be available on the word processor, such as automatic word division, forced line endings, format lines to change line spacing, and superior or

inferior carriage shifts. Most of these computer-specific commands will not translate onto typesetting machines and will result in added time and expense. Again, communication with the publisher will help avoid many of these conversion problems.

3. The average word-processing software, like the old-fashioned typewriter, uses only one kind of quote mark at the beginning and end of a quotation. In phototypesetting, however, open quotes are carefully distinguished from close quotes. The publisher's list of typesetting codes and special characters will instruct the author in the proper insertion of these marks.

4. Many typists are in the habit of using a lower-case *el* (l) for the numeral *one* (1). In typesetting, the el and the one must be carefully distinguished. The author should not resort to the typist's habit of interchanging these characters.

5. The same problem arises with the *oh* (O) and the *zero* (0). Again the author should always be careful to type the intended character.

6. Many typists and word-processor users type a title, a running head, or the author's name at the top of every manuscript page. When a disk is intended for typesetting, this practice should be avoided since the typesetter will only have to eliminate such extraneous data. This applies to typed page numbers (*folios*) as well.

7. Footnotes can also be problematic. Many older style manuals recommend that the author type all footnote references at the bottom of the manuscript page on which the reference is to appear (simulating its position when typeset). This was convenient for typewritten manuscripts, but computer typesetting systems can most efficiently handle footnotes when set together at the end of the book or chapter, corresponding sequentially to the superscript numbers in the text. The computer

can then format all the footnotes at one time and insert them into the printed text where needed.

8. When the author is in doubt concerning a compound word—whether it should be set as two words, hyphenated, or set solid—it is best to set it solid so that the publisher's computerized spelling checker will be more apt to catch it if it is wrong. If typed as two words or hyphenated, the spelling checker may allow both words individually but miss the fact that they should have been set solid.

Other considerations. Many writers, enthusiastic about the advancements in word processing, have bought systems to replace their typewriters. Although the word processor made editing and revision easier, it did not necessarily improve the quality of the end product: the typed copy. Every writer who plans to use the word processor to produce paper copy should obtain as good a letter-quality printer as is affordable. Although many of the early printers, with their broken dot-matrix letters, have been replaced by more sophisticated machines, the author should still ask, "Is my printer an aesthetic improvement over my old typewriter?" Publishers, perhaps, have complained too strenuously about the unreadability of some printing systems, but the question remains: How much is a writer willing to sacrifice for the convenience of computerization?

B. The Publisher's Computer

For many book companies, the effects of computerization have been limited to the typesetting room where computerized typesetting systems are common. The editors in such companies still edit in the traditional manner—on paper. Since the development of printing, editing has been a process that leaves a discernible trail of more or less clearly marked revisions, insertions, and deletions. The editor left tracks.

But many editors now edit in an entirely new way. We are now in the later stages of a transition to computer editing. In many publishing companies, the computers themselves often search for and correct common punctuation, spelling, and grammar errors, leaving the editor free to consider the larger style questions like structure and organization. Content and copy editors commonly work directly on VDTs (video-display terminals). We are seeing the rise of a generation of editors, in fact, who, having been trained on the word processor, have had little experience in applying a blue pencil to paper. And again, while technology has facilitated the editing process, other aspects of traditional book editing have been sacrificed.

For example, the traditional editor used to return the marked and edited paper manuscript to the author so that the author could review all the changes and respond to the editor's queries. But this courtesy has now become less common. Since manuscripts are now often edited entirely on the computer, the editor usually replaces old matter with new; the original version, at that point, ceases to exist. Traditionally, corrections on paper were written around, between, over, and next to the original copy, but the old could still be easily compared with the new. But insert and delete symbols cannot be rendered on a computer.

As a result, many authors are surprised and frustrated to receive from their editor a revised version of their manuscript (often at proof stage) with no detailed annotation of the specific changes that were made. If the author desires to see how editing has altered the original, he or she must proofread the edited version against a copy of the original. Some people have suggested that editors might avoid this problem by annotating a paper copy of the manuscript as the editing changes are being made on screen. This, of course, defeats the labor-saving benefit of editing on the computer in the first place; if forced to annotate all changes on paper, the editor would save more time by eliminating the computer altogether.

There are no perfect solutions. Experimental software exists that indicates on a print-out all editing changes—this new software, in effect, shows the insert and delete symbols. The software, however, is expensive, of limited value, and not likely to come into common use any time in the near future. Although the time constraints of publishing may not allow the application of the following solutions, some of these suggestions may be helpful:

1. Communication between editor and author is essential. As the editing begins, both in-house and free-lance editors should jot down any general editorial principles that are being applied: such as, curbing any problems with the passive voice, revising sexist language, major change in reference style, and so on. In this way the author can be informed about the kinds of changes to expect.

2. The editor can annotate a single chapter of the book on a paper copy and send it to the author. Although this will not show the editor's changes for the entire book, it will at least familiarize the author with the general editorial style and allow the author to respond.

3. The editor can annotate many major changes on the computer manuscript itself, which can then be printed out on a high-speed character printer and sent to the author for approval. These annotations are flagged in such a way (by typing them in all caps or in brackets or with special coding) that they can be easily removed before typesetting. Flagged annotations must be removed, however, before the copy is typeset since even a single annotation can throw off the page count of an entire book.

4. The final and most common option is for the editor to send the author a copy of the first proofs, with notes attached concerning the general style decisions that were made. This puts added pressure on the author, because, without specific annotations, the author must read the proofs carefully to detect many of the subtle changes that may have been made.

The problems inherent in this system mean that the author and editor must work even more closely together in the early stages of editing so that both are aware of any areas that will need heavy editing and both feel comfortable with the limitations of computer-based book processing.

The author should also be aware of the significance of the strange symbols that often appear on a publisher's print-out of the book. These are the computer codes that communicate all matters of type and spacing to the typesetting machine. Such codes as *P1, -/p-, or -p- (all of which indicate that a paragraph is to begin in various computer typesetting programs) will be printed out when a paper copy is made from a computer manuscript. In general these should not interfere with reading, and they can be readily interpreted from the context of the words they accompany. Occasionally when special symbols or marks are required, codes may appear in what seem to be odd places, but again the context should at least indicate that some sort of special symbol is needed. It is the editor's, copy editor's, and typesetter's responsibility to check the coding of each manuscript, not the author's.

In proofs, a *broken code* may occasionally appear in the text. That is, when an incorrect code has been used, the typesetter will often "spit out" the characters of the broken code. Although the results can be damaging to the appearance of the proofs, it is usually a simple matter to correct the code on the next set of proofs.

C. The Proofreader

Not long ago many proofreaders feared they were soon destined for extinction. Computerized dictionaries and spelling checkers, they were told, would soon do to them what the IBM personal computer had done to the Underwood typewriter. With the flush of confidence that accompanied the rise of the computer industry, many writers in the field of publishing even advocated the abolition of the entire proofreading profession.

Now, twenty years into the computer publishing revolution, proofreaders remain as invaluable as ever, although their function has been modified in some interesting and unexpected ways.

For instance, many companies now employ in-house staff

to proofread manuscripts on the VDT itself. Such proofreaders combine traditional functions, such as checking for correct spelling and punctuation, with newer computerized functions, such as checking typesetting codes and managing spelling-checker software. Many publishers, though, have not been pleased with the accuracy of on-screen proofing. Furthermore, many format problems can only be readily identified in type.

Although paper is still the most common medium for proofreading, many changes have taken place. The most noticeable has been the shift from double- to single-copy proofreading.

Traditionally, a proofreader compared the newly typeset galleys (*live copy*) against an edited manuscript (*dead copy*). Now that many editors and copy editors perform their functions on the VDT screen, no authoritative paper copy exists to show all the changes that have been made. Computerization has rung the death knell of dead copy.

The proofreader, therefore, must become proficient at *straight proofreading* (also called "railroading"), which is reading galley proofs with no manuscript against which to check. Straight proofreading can actually be more accurate because it allows the proofreader's eyes to focus solely on the live copy and eliminates the fatigue of constantly having to shift 'the eyes between two copies. Still, many proofreaders tend to speed up when reading straight copy, a tendency that results in greater inaccuracy. In any case, this new way of proofreading has made new demands on the proofreader.

Traditional proofreaders, when asked to read straight copy, are often frustrated by not having a manuscript against which to read. They are now required to know more; they need to think more like editors by understanding just what an author intends to say, but they must also maintain their obsession with detail. The guides available to them to answer their questions are the following: (1) a dictionary, (2) a style manual, (3) a style sheet or other information provided by the editor, and (4) common sense.

1. *Dictionary*. Most proofreaders who read straight copy find they use the dictionary far more than when they were reading against dead copy. Proofreaders should get into the habit of looking up every word, even the most common, that they are not completely certain how to spell. The proofreader should obtain a copy of the publisher's preferred dictionary and use it often.

2. *Style manual*. Most publishers conform to one of many popular manuals of style, such as the *Chicago Manual of Style* or *Words Into Type*. They will also commonly provide proofreaders with their own in-house style guides that summarize major rules and indicate variations from their chosen manual of style. The proofreader must be certain to have access to and be thoroughly familiar with all these references.

3. *The style sheet*. Since editors do not have a paper manuscript on which to indicate style decisions (for instance, whether to capitalize the deity pronoun or to use the serial comma), a style sheet should be used to inform a proofreader of these decisions, especially when they depart from the publisher's accepted dictionary or manual of style. Style sheets have always been an important strategy for communicating style decisions to everyone involved in a manuscript's development; style sheets are even more important for the proofreader of straight copy. The proofreader too should keep a style sheet to annotate all questions of fact, style, spelling, and grammar that might recur.

4. *Common sense*. Proofreaders proficient at straight reading will tell you that they have had to develop a certain caginess. They learn to read with the "flow" of the manuscript. Even when no style sheet is provided, they can still figure out where variations from accepted style were deliberately made. In a sense, they learn to second-guess both the author and the editor, though this, in turn, can lead to the added problem of incorrect second-

guesses. The straight proofreader must learn when it is necessary to query. With no authoritative manuscript, the potential exists for proofreaders to query too often, when in fact they might be able to answer their own questions by reading further in the manuscript.

An overview of how the publisher handles computerized editing and typesetting is essential to the proofreader. In fact, proofreaders should insist that the publisher provide a brief sketch of the company's editing and production process. This will allow proofreaders to adapt to the system and even devise ways of facilitating their own procedures. For instance, if the proofreader is aware that the editor uses a word-processing system with a search function, the proofreader can keep a list of problematic words to be searched for consistency. Or the proofreader may need to know whether the copy to be proofed is a print-quality galley or simply a rough emulation. Emulations are adequate for checking typographical problems but are usually not of high enough quality for printing. It wastes the proofreader's time to check for broken letters or kerning on an emulation that is only an approximation of the final copy.

The better the proofreader can understand computerized publishing, the better the proofreader will be able to avoid some of the new hazards of computerization—for instance, word division. Most proofreaders are aware that many dictionaries differ on the question of where to properly hyphenate some words. Style manuals, furthermore, regard only certain dictionary word divisions as legitimate for typesetting purposes. Add to this the fact that phototypesetters generate their own word divisions in two ways: from the computer's own programmed dictionary memory and by a logic program, neither of which may necessarily correspond to the dictionary that the publishing house and proofreader are using. To sort out all this confusion, a few rules may be helpful.

1. Conform first to CMS style of word division (CMS 6.33–6.47). These rules cover those words that the typesetting computer has broken by "logic." These rules also define

which dictionary breaks are and are not legitimate for typesetting purposes.

2. In addition to CMS, some publishers accept any word division that conforms to the style of any major dictionary. For instance, *righteous* may be broken either *righteous* (*Webster's*) or *right-eous* (*Random House*). This liberality is often a compromise of style and quality. In many cases, however, it is a necessity, since even a slight adjustment in line length can cause a paragraph, chapter, or even an entire book to rejustify. Little adjustments can snowball into expensive major changes. Proofreaders should be sure to understand the publisher's style of word division; a book's editor should be able to provide the proofreader with this information.

In spite of such difficulties, computerized typesetting has eliminated many of the problems traditional proofreaders used to encounter. For instance, such machines will never invert a character (except for quotation marks), and the better-quality equipment will rarely produce a broken or chipped character. It may, however, spit out a *broken code* (a computer code that is incorrectly used, which may or may not show up in the typeset copy) and *garbage* (the typeset result of a broken code). It is not uncommon to see an entire sentence or paragraph set in a wrong font or in garbled characters as the result of a mistyped code. The proofreader must be careful to distinguish between what is a coding problem and what is intended.

Many proofreaders have discovered that computer typesetters tend to repeat their mistakes, which means the proofreader may have to be more assertive and willing to query. If a computer code was accidentally programmed to typeset an incorrect typeface, then that code will result in the wrong typeface each time it is used. The proofreader should not necessarily accept an odd design element just because it is set consistently throughout the book.

Another problem for the proofreader is *flags* (an editor's, author's, or typesetter's annotations that are not intended to be part of the final book). Often a proofreader will assume that these obvious flags will be searched and caught by the editor or typesetter when, in fact, these flags were already missed. The proofreader should mark anything, no matter how obvious, that is not intended to appear in print. An example: suppose that a special dingbat is to be used in the text; the editor might type a note that states, "XXX Note: Dingbat to go here XXX." The proofreader should not assume that this note will be caught; he or she should call it to the editor's attention.

While proofreading used to be a fairly mechanical operation, it now allows room for much more creative problem solving. While maintaining their discretion, proofreaders must think more like copy editors and sometimes even like designers. They must know when to query without querying too much and when to make corrections in punctuation, position, and grammar without arrogating the editor's role.

Unfortunately, many observers agree that computerization has not led to better quality books. Most people who appreciate good books feel that standards are on the decline, that more typos are appearing in print than ever. The irony is that, when not used wisely, computers can contribute to the problem.

To help the proofreader become more wise to these problems, here are a few tips for reading proofs generated on a phototypesetter.

1. Avoid the temptation to speed up when reading a single copy. Some proofreaders even read aloud to keep from going too fast. Read word-for-word as in traditional proofreading, look up all unfamiliar words, and check them letter-for-letter.

2. Avoid the temptation to get caught up in the story. Not only do straight-proofreaders tend to speed up, but because they are focusing more closely on a single copy, a kind of hypnosis can occur. Proofreaders can easily become so absorbed in a narrative that they will wake up four pages later to realize that they haven't been looking for errors.

3. Take at least a five-minute break every hour. And remember: straight proofreading can be even more intense than traditional proofreading.

4. Keep a style sheet. Note all unusual words and names and any special grammar, punctuation, abbreviation, or symbol considerations. Also keep track of fonts, leadings, and specification changes if the publisher has not provided a specification sheet or cast-off.

5. Be particularly careful about font changes. When italic material is called for, use common sense to ascertain where the italics are to end. Sometimes they will erroneously extend into copy that should be roman.

6. Double-check all folios to make sure they are all in the same font. Many phototypesetting machines will inadvertently set the folio number in the same font as the last word on the page. If that word is reduced or italicized, the folio may match it and needs to be marked "wrong font."

No doubt, computers will become even more important to publishing in the nineties and in the twenty-first century. Whether computerization will make for better Christian books in the future is entirely in the hands of the writers, the editors, the proofreaders, and ultimately the readers of today's religious books.

APPENDIXES

Appendix A: Additional Resources

This manual has tried to focus on resource materials for writers and editors of religious books. While it provides general rules of style and usage, much related information is beyond the scope of this manual. This appendix provides a quick reference guide for some of this information. The following are the standard references and abbreviations used:

CMS   *The Chicago Manual of Style.* Thirteenth edition.
WEB   *Webster's Ninth New Collegiate Dictionary.*
WIT   *Words Into Type. Third Edition.*

Appendix B: Holidays, Feasts, and the Liturgical Year

Many of the following holidays are not recognized by some denominations. Most Protestant churches, for instance, do not celebrate saints' days. The following list shows those holidays that have had historical importance to some portion of the orthodox church.

A. Advent

One of the two major seasons in the church calendar, Advent spans the period between Advent Sunday and Christmas. Advent (from Latin *adventus*, meaning "coming") is the season of remembering Christ's nativity and, by extension, his second coming.

1. Advent Sunday. In Western churches, Advent begins on the fourth Sunday before Christmas. That Sunday is generally considered the beginning of the church year.
2. Christmas (December 25). The day on which the birth, or nativity, of Christ is commemorated.

B. Epiphany (January 6)

Epiphany is the celebration of Christ's manifestation to the Magi and to the gentile world in general. This is a particularly important holiday in the Eastern church, where it is the commemoration of Christ's baptism.

C. Lent

The primary church season, Lent is traditionally a period of fasting and penance commemorated between Ash Wednesday and Easter. All dates in the Lenten season are established in relation to Easter, the date of which is determined by calculating the first Sunday after the paschal full moon, and can fall on or between March 21 and April 25.

1. Shrove Tuesday. The day before Ash Wednesday; generally a time of preparation for Lent. Outside the church, the day is better known as Mardi Gras, the traditional day of feasting before the Lenten fast.
2. Ash Wednesday. A day of penance. The official beginning of Lent. It is forty days (not counting Sundays) before Easter.
3. Palm Sunday, or Passion Sunday. The Sunday before Easter, on which Christ's triumphant entry into Jerusalem is remembered. The seven-day period beginning on Palm Sunday is called Holy Week.
4. Maundy Thursday. The Thursday before Easter, traditionally the day on which Christ's institution of the sacrament of Communion is commemorated.
5. Good Friday. The Friday before Easter. On this day Christ's crucifixion and death are remembered.
6. Easter Sunday. The celebration of Christ's resurrection. The following chart shows the dates for Ash Wednesday and Easter.

Dates of Ash Wednesday and Easter

Year	Ash Wednesday	Easter
1989	February 8	March 26
1990	February 28	April 15
1991	February 13	March 31
1992	March 4	April 19

1993	February 24	April 11
1994	February 16	April 3
1995	March 1	April 16
1996	February 21	April 7
1997	February 12	March 30
1998	February 25	April 12
1999	February 17	April 4
2000	March 8	April 23
2001	February 28	April 15
2002	February 13	March 31
2003	March 5	April 20
2004	February 25	April 11
2005	February 9	March 27
2006	March 1	April 16
2007	February 21	April 8
2008	February 6	March 23
2009	February 25	April 12
2010	February 17	April 4
2011	March 9	April 24
2012	February 22	April 8
2013	February 13	March 31
2014	March 5	April 20
2015	February 18	April 5
2016	February 10	March 27
2017	March 1	April 16
2018	February 14	April 1
2019	March 6	April 21
2020	February 26	April 12
2021	February 17	April 4
2022	March 2	April 17
2023	February 22	April 9
2024	February 14	March 31
2025	March 5	April 20

D. Pentecost

This is celebrated on the seventh Sunday after Easter and commemorates the descent of the Holy Spirit on the apostles. Pentecost Sunday is also called Whitsunday in England.

E. Trinity Sunday

This day is set aside to honor the Trinity and is celebrated the Sunday after Pentecost.

F. Other Christian Holidays and Feast Days

Week of Prayer for Christian Unity (January 18 to 25)
Conversion of Saint Paul (January 25)
Presentation of Christ, or Candlemas (February 2)
Annunciation (March 25)
Ascension Day (the fifth Thursday after Easter)
Nativity of John the Baptist (June 24)
Feast of Saint Peter and Saint Paul (June 29)
Visitation (July 2)
Transfiguration of Our Lord (August 6)
Michaelmas (September 29)
Worldwide Communion Sunday (first Sunday in October)
Reformation Sunday (last Sunday in October)
Reformation Day (October 31)
All Saints' Day (November 1)
All Souls' Day (November 2)
Saint Lucy's Day, or Santa Lucia (December 13)
Saint Stephen's Day (December 26)
Holy Innocents' Day (December 28)

G. Major Dates of the Jewish Year

Purim (Feast of Esther)
Pesach (Passover)
Shabuoth (Pentecost)
Rosh Hashanah (Jewish New Year)
Yom Kippur (Day of Atonement)
Sukkoth (Feast of Booths)
Hanukkah (Feast of the Dedication)

Appendix C:
U.S. Denominations and Associations of Churches

Adventist
 Advent Christian Church
 Church of God General Conference
 Seventh-day Adventist
African Orthodox Church
Amana Church Society
American Ethical Union
American Evangelical Christian Churches
American Rescue Workers
Anglican Orthodox Church
Apostolic Christian Church (Nazarean)
Apostolic Christian Church of America
Apostolic Faith
Apostolic Overcoming Holy Church of God
Armenian Apostolic Church of America, Eastern Prelacy
Armenian Churches

Baha'i
Baptist
 American Baptist Association
 American Baptist Churches in the U.S.A.
 Baptist Bible Fellowship, International
 Baptist General Conference

Baptist Missionary Association of America
Bethel Ministerial Association
Black Baptist
Central Baptist Association
Conservative Baptist Association of America
Duck River (and Kindred) Association of Baptists (Baptist Church
    of Christ)
Free Will Baptist
General Association of Regular Baptist Churches
General Baptist
General Conference of the Evangelical Baptist Church, Inc.
Landmark Baptist
National Baptist Evangelical Life and Soul Saving Assembly of
    the U.S.A.
National Primitive Baptist Convention of the U.S.A.
North American Baptist Conference
Primitive Baptist
Reformed Baptist
Separate Baptists in Christ (General Association of Separate
    Baptists)
Seventh Day Baptist General Conference
Southern Baptist Convention
Two-Seed-in-the-Spirit Predestinarian Baptist
United Baptist
United Free Will Baptist
Berean Fundamental Church
Bible Fellowship Church
Bible Protestant Church
Bible Way Church, Worldwide
Black Muslim
Brethren
    Dunkers
        Brethren Church (Ashland)
        Church of the Brethren
        Fellowship of Grace Brethren Churches
        Old German Baptist Brethren (Old Order Dunkers)
    River Brethren
        Brethren in Christ Church (formerly River Brethren)
        Old Order (Yorker) Brethren
        United Zion Church
    United Brethren

Church of the United Brethren in Christ
Buddhist Churches of America

Christadelphian
Christian and Missionary Alliance
Christian Catholic Church
Christian Church (Disciples of Christ)
Christian Church of North America, General Council of
Christian Churches and Churches of Christ
Christian Congregation
Christian Union
Christ's Sanctified Holy Church
Church of Christ (Holiness) U.S.A.
Church of Christ, Scientist
Church of God
   Church of God (Huntsville, Alabama)
   Church of God, Inc. (Original)
   Church of God (Anderson, Indiana)
   Church of God (Cleveland, Tennessee)
   Church of God (Seventh Day)
   Church of God and Saints of Christ
   Church of God by Faith, Inc.
   Church of God in Christ
   Church of God in Christ (International)
   The Church of God of Prophecy
Church of Illumination
Church of Jesus Christ
Church of Our Lord Jesus Christ of the Apostolic Faith, Inc.
Church of the Nazarene
Churches of Christ
Churches of Christ in Christian Union
Churches of God, General Conference
Churches of God, Holiness
Churches of the Living God
Community Churches, National Council of
Congregational Bible Holiness Church
Congregational Christian Churches (National Association)
Congregational Holiness Church
Conservative Congregational Christian Conference

Divine Science

Episcopal
  Episcopal Church
  Reformed Episcopal Church
Evangelical Christian Churches
Evangelical Church of North America
Evangelical Congregational Church
Evangelical Covenant Church of America
Evangelical Free Church of America
Evangelical Orthodox

Fire-Baptized Holiness Church
Foursquare Gospel, International Church of the
Free Christian Zion Church of Christ
Friends (Quaker)
  Friends General Conference
  Friends United Meeting (Five Years Meeting)
  Religious Society of Friends (Conservative)

Grace Gospel Fellowship

Independent Fundamental Churches of America

Jehovah's Witnesses
Judaism
  Conservative Judaism
  Orthodox Judaism
  Reconstructionism
  Reform Judaism

Kodesh Church of Immanuel

Latter-Day Saints (Mormon)
  Church of Christ (Temple Lot)
  Church of Jesus Christ (Bickertonites)
  Church of Jesus Christ of Latter-Day Saints
  Church of Jesus Christ of Latter-Day Saints (Strangite)
  Reorganized Church of Jesus Christ of Latter-Day Saints
Liberal Catholic Church
Lutheran
  American Lutheran Church
  Apostolic Lutheran Church of America
  Church of the Lutheran Brethren of America

Church of the Lutheran Confession
Evangelical Lutheran Synod
Free Lutheran Congregations, The Association of
Lutheran Church–Missouri Synod
Protestant Conference (Lutheran)
Wisconsin Evangelical Lutheran Synod

Mennonite
Beachy Amish Mennonite Churches
Church of God in Christ, Mennonite
Conservative Mennonite Conference
Evangelical Mennonite Brethren Conference
Evangelical Mennonite Church
General Conference Mennonite Church
Hutterian Brethren
Mennonite Brethren Church of North America
Mennonite Church
Old Order Amish Church
Old Order (Wisler) Mennonite Church
Reformed Mennonite Church
Unaffiliated Mennonite
Methodist
African Methodist Episcopal Church
African Methodist Episcopal Zion Church
African Union First Colored Methodist Protestant Church, Inc.
Christian Methodist Episcopal Church
Congregational Methodist Church
Evangelical Methodist Church
First Congregational Methodist Church of the U.S.A.
Free Methodist Church of North America
New Congregational Methodist Church
People's Methodist Church
Primitive Methodist Church, U.S.A.
Reformed Methodist Union Episcopal Church
Reformed Zion Union Apostolic Church
Southern Methodist Church
Union American Methodist Episcopal Church
United Methodist Church
Metropolitan Community Churches, Universal Fellowship of
Missionary Church
Moravian

Moravian
  Moravian Church (Unitas Fratrum)
  Unity of the Brethren
Muslim

New Apostolic Church of North America

Old Catholic
  American Catholic Church (Syro-Antiochian)
  Mariavite Old Catholic Church
  North American Old Roman Catholic Churches
  Old Roman Catholic Church (English Rite)
Open Bible Standard Churches, Inc.
Orthodox (Eastern)
  Albanian Orthodox Archdiocese in America
  American Carpatho-Russian Orthodox
  Greek Catholic Church
  American Holy Orthodox Catholic Eastern Church
  Antiochian Orthodox Christian Archdiocese of North America
  Bulgarian Eastern Orthodox Church
  Greek Orthodox Archdiocese of North and South America
  Holy Apostolic and Catholic Church of the East (Assyrian)
  Romanian Orthodox Episcopate of America
  Russian Orthodox Church
  Serbian Eastern Orthodox Church in the U.S.A. and Canada
  Syrian Orthodox Church of Antioch (Archdiocese of the U.S.A.
      and Canada)
  Ukrainian Orthodox Churches

Pentecostal
  Assemblies of God, General Council of
  Calvary Pentecostal Church, Inc.
  Elim Fellowship
  Emmanuel Holiness Church
  Independent Assemblies of God, International
  International Pentecostal Church of Christ
  International Pentecostal Holiness Church
  Pentecostal Assemblies of the World, Inc.
  Pentecostal Church of God
  Pentecostal Free-Will Baptist Church
  United Pentecostal Church International
  Pillar of Fire

Plymouth Brethren
Polish National Catholic Church of America
Presbyterian
   Associate Reformed Presbyterian Church
   Bible Presbyterian Church
   Cumberland Presbyterian Church
   Orthodox Presbyterian Church
   Presbyterian Church (U.S.A.)
   Presbyterian Church in America
   Reformed Presbyterian Church of North America
   Second Cumberland Presbyterian Church in the United States

Reformed
   Christian Reformed Church
   Hungarian Reformed Church in America
   Netherlands Reformed Congregations
   Protestant Reformed Churches in America
   Reformed Church in America
   Reformed Church in the United States
Roman Catholic Church

Salvation Army
Schwenkfelder Church
Social Brethren
Spiritualist
   International General Assembly of Spiritualists
   National Spiritual Alliance of the U.S.A.
   National Spiritualist Association of Churches
   Progressive Spiritual Church
Swedenborgian (The New Jerusalem)

Theosophy
Triumph the Church and Kingdom of God in Christ

Unitarian Universalist Association
United Church of Christ
   Congregational Church
   Christian Church
   Evangelical and Reformed Church
United Holy Church of America, Inc.
Unity School of Christianity

Universal Christian Spiritual Faith and Churches of All Nations

Vedanta Society
Volunteers of America

Wesleyan Church
Worldwide Church of God

REFERENCES

A. Standard References

The Chicago Manual of Style. 13th ed. Chicago: University of Chicago Press, 1982.

The NIV Study Bible. Grand Rapids: Zondervan, 1985.

12,000 Words: A Supplement to Webster's Third New International Dictionary. Springfield, Mass.: Merriam-Webster, 1986.

Webster's Ninth New Collegiate Dictionary. Springfield, Mass.: Merriam-Webster, 1985.

B. English Usage, Style, and Grammar

Bernstein, Theodore M. The Careful Writer: A Modern Guide to English Usage. New York: Atheneum, 1965.

_____. Dos, Don'ts & Maybes of English Usage. New York: Times Books, 1977.

_____. Miss Thistlebottom's Hobgoblins: The Careful Writer's Guide to the Taboos, Bugbears and Outmoded Rules of English Usage. New York: Simon and Schuster, 1984.

Copperud, Roy H. American Usage and Style: The Consensus. New York: Van Nostrand Reinhold, 1979.

Curme, George O. English Grammar. New York: Barnes & Noble, 1967.

Fernald, James C. English Grammar Simplified. New York: Barnes & Noble, 1979.

Follett, Wilson. *Modern American Usage: A Guide.* Edited and completed by Jacques Barzun and others. New York: Hill and Wang, 1966.

Fowler, H. W. *A Dictionary of Modern English Usage.* 2d ed. London: Oxford University Press, 1983.

Gordon, Karen Elizabeth. *The Transitive Vampire: A Handbook of Grammar for the Innocent, the Eager, and the Doomed.* New York: Times Books, 1984.

_____. *The Well-Tempered Sentence: A Punctuation Handbook for the Innocent, the Eager, and the Doomed.* New Haven: Ticknor and Fields, 1983.

Johnson, Edward D. *The Handbook of Good English.* New York: Facts on File, 1982.

Morris, William, and Mary Morris. *Harper Dictionary of Contemporary Usage.* 2d ed. New York: Harper & Row, 1985.

Opdycke, John B. *Harper's English Grammar.* New York: Warner Books, 1983.

Paxson, William C. *The Mentor Guide to Punctuation.* New York, Mentor Books/New American Library, 1986.

Shaw, Harry. *Punctuate It Right!* New York: Harper & Row, 1963.

_____. *Errors in English and Ways to Correct Them.* 3d ed. New York: Harper & Row, 1986.

Shertzer, Margaret. *The Elements of Grammar.* New York: Macmillan, 1986.

Strunk, William, Jr., and E. B. White. *The Elements of Style.* 3d ed. New York: Macmillan, 1979.

Success With Words: A Guide to the American Language. Pleasantville, N.Y.: Reader's Digest Association, 1983.

Words Into Type. 3d ed. Englewood Cliffs, N.J.: Prentice-Hall, 1974.

C. Writing, Revising, and Editing

1. General

Appelbaum, Judith, and Nancy Evans. *How to Get Happily Published.* New York: Harper & Row, 1978.

Atchity, Kenneth. *A Writer's Time: A Guide to the Creative Process, From Vision Through Revision.* New York: W. W. Norton, 1986.

Barzun, Jacques. *On Writing, Editing and Publishing.* 2d ed. Chicago: University of Chicago Press, 1986.

_____. *Simple and Direct: A Rhetoric for Writers.* Rev. ed. New York: Harper & Row, 1984.

Boston, Bruce O., ed. *STET! Tricks of the Trade for Writers and Editors.* Alexandria, Va.: Editorial Experts, 1986.

Boswell, John. *The Awful Truth About Publishing: Why They Always Reject Your Manuscript . . . and What You Can Do About It.* New York: Warner Books, 1986.

Cheney, Theodore A. Rees. *Getting the Words Right: How to Revise, Edit and Rewrite.* Cincinnati: Writer's Digest Books, 1983.

Flesch, Rudolf. *The Art of Readable Writing.* Rev. ed. New York: Harper & Row, 1974.

Graves, Robert, and Alan Hodge. *The Reader Over Your Shoulder: A Handbook for Writers of English Prose.* 2d ed. New York: Random House, 1979.

Gunning, Robert. *The Technique of Clear Writing.* Rev. ed. New York: McGraw-Hill, 1968.

Plotnik, Arthur. *The Elements of Editing: A Modern Guide for Editors and Journalists.* New York: Macmillan, 1982.

Read, Herbert. *English Prose Style.* New York: Pantheon Books, 1952.

Stainton, Elsie Myers. *Author and Editor at Work: Making a Better Book.* Toronto: University of Toronto Press, 1982.

Zinsser, William. *On Writing Well: An Informal Guide to Writing Nonfiction.* 3d ed. New York: Harper & Row, 1985.

2. Religious

Anderson, Margaret J. *The Christian Writer's Handbook.* Rev. ed. New York: Harper & Row, 1983.

Aycock, Don M., and Leonard George Goss. *Writing Religiously: A Guide to Writing Nonfiction Religious Books.* Grand Rapids: Baker, 1984.

_____. *Inside Religious Publishing.* Grand Rapids: Zondervan, to be published in 1989.

Gentz, William H. *The Religious Writer's Marketplace: The Definitive Sourcebook.* Rev. ed. Philadelphia: Running Press, 1985.

Gentz, William, et al. *Writing to Inspire: A Guide to Writing and Publishing for the Expanding Religious Market.* Cincinnati: Writer's Digest Books, 1982.

Herr, Ethel. *An Introduction to Christian Writing.* Wheaton, Ill.: Tyndale House, 1983.

McCarthy, David S. *Practical Guide for the Christian Writer*. Valley Forge, Pa.: Judson Press, 1983.

Schell, Mildred. *Wanted: Writers for the Christian Market*. Valley Forge, Penn.: Judson Press, 1975.

Spencer, Sue Nichols. *Words on Target: For Better Christian Communication*. Richmond: John Knox Press, 1964.

Wirt, Sherwood E. *Getting Into Print*. Nashville: Nelson, 1977.

_____. *The Making of a Writer: A Christian Writer's Guide*. Minneapolis: Augsburg, 1987.

D. Special Aspects of Writing and Editing

1. Copy editing and proofreading

Butcher, Judith. *Copy-editing: The Cambridge Handbook*. New York: Cambridge University Press, 1975.

Judd, Karen. *Copyediting: A Practical Guide*. Los Altos, Calif.: William Kaufmann, 1982.

McNaughton, Harry H. *Proofreading and Copyediting*. New York: Hastings House, 1973.

Smith, Peggy. *Mark My Words: Instruction and Practice in Proofreading*. Alexandria, Va.: Editorial Experts, 1987.

_____. *Simplified Proofreading*. Alexandria, Va.: Editorial Experts, 1984.

2. Gender-specific language

Equality in Print: A Guide for Editors and Publishers. Chicago: Chicago Women in Publishing, 1978.

Guidelines for Creating Positive Sexual and Racial Images in Educational Materials. New York: Macmillan, 1975.

Maggio, Rosalie, *The Nonsexist Word Finder: A Dictionary of Gender-Free Usage*. Phoenix: Oryx, 1987.

Miller, Casey, and Kate Swift. *The Handbook of Nonsexist Writing*. New York: Lippincott and Crowell, 1980.

Supplement to the Publication Manual of the American Psychological Association. 2d ed. Washington, D.C.: APA, 1974.

Wiley Guidelines on Sexism in Language. New York: John Wiley and Sons, 1977.

3. Indexing

Collison, Robert L. *Indexing Books*. Rev. ed. Tuckahoe, N.Y.: John de Graff, 1967.

Spiker, Sina. *Indexing Your Book: A Practical Guide for Authors*. Madison: University of Wisconsin Press, 1954.

4. Writing and word processing

An Author's Primer to Word Processing. New York: Association of American Publishers, 1983.

Chicago Guide to Preparing Electronic Manuscripts. Chicago: University of Chicago Press, 1987.

McWilliams, Peter A. *The Word Processing Book: A Short Course in Computer Literacy.* New York: Ballantine/Prelude Press, 1982.

Zinsser, William. *Writing With a Word Processor.* New York: Harper & Row, 1983.

5. Copyright

Johnston, Donald F. *Copyright Handbook.* New York: R. R. Bowker, 1978.

Nimmer, Melville B. *Nimmer on Copyright: Literary, Musical, Artistic Property.* 4 vols. New York: Matthew Bender. Continually updated.

Strong, William S. *The Copyright Book: A Practical Guide.* Cambridge: MIT Press, 1984.

E. The Publishing Business

Adler, Bill. *Inside Publishing.* Indianapolis: Bobbs-Merrill, 1982.

Bailey, Herbert S., Jr. *The Art and Science of Book Publishing.* Austin: University of Texas Press, 1970.

Balkin, Richard. *A Writer's Guide to Book Publishing.* Revised and expanded edition. New York: Hawthorn/Dutton, 1981.

Brownstone, David M., and Irene M. Franck. *The Dictionary of Publishing.* New York: Van Nostrand Reinhold, 1982.

Current Christian Books. Colorado Springs: Christian Booksellers Association Service Corporation. Published annually.

Dessauer, John P. *Book Publishing: What It Is, What It Does.* 2d ed. New York: R. R. Bowker, 1981.

Duke, Judith S. *Religious Publishing and Communications.* White Plains, N.Y.: Knowledge and Industry Publications, 1981.

Lee, Marshall. *Bookmaking: The Illustrated Guide to Design, Production, Editing.* Rev. ed. New York: R. R. Bowker, 1980.

Literary Market Place (LMP). New York: R. R. Bowker. Published annually.

Polking, Kirk, ed. *Writer's Encyclopedia.* Cincinnati: Writer's Digest Books, 1983.

Shatzkin, Leonard. *In Cold Type: Overcoming the Book Crisis.* Boston: Houghton Mifflin, 1982.

F. Journals for Writers and Editors

1. General trade magazines

The Editorial Eye. Newsletter on style, usage, and professional standards published by Editorial Experts, Inc., 85 S. Bragg St., Alexandria, VA 22312-2731.

Publishers Weekly: The International News Magazine of Book Publishing. Published by the Cahners Publishing Company, 249 W. 17th St., New York, NY 10011.

Righting Words: The Journal of Language and Editing. Published by the Righting Words Corporation, 425 E. 65th St., New York, NY 10021.

Scholarly Publishing. Journal published quarterly by the University of Toronto Press, Toronto, Canada M52 1A6.

Small Press: The Magazine for Independent/In-House/Desktop Publishing. Published by the Meckler Corporation, P.O. Box 3000, Denville, NJ 07834.

2. For writers and editors of religious books

Books & Religion: A Quarterly Review. Trinity Church, 74 Trinity Place, New York, NY 10006-2088.

Bookstore Journal. The official publication of the Christian Booksellers Association, 2620 Venetucci Blvd., P.O. Box 200, Colorado Springs, CO 80901.

The Inspirational Writer. Writer's Digest, 1507 Dana Ave., Cincinnati, OH 45207.

Christianity and Literature. Calvin College, Grand Rapids, MI 49506.

G. Suppliers of Books on Writing, Editing, and Publishing

Editorial Experts, Inc., 85 Bragg Street, Alexandria, VA 22312-2731. (Supplies their own newsletter, *The Editorial Eye,* and their own publications for editors and proofreaders.)

mehitabel s, P.O. Box 60357, Palo Alto, CA 94306. (General books for writers and editors.)

Ross Book Service, 3718 Seminary Road, Seminary PO, Alexandria, VA 22304-0993. (General books for writers and editors.)

Subject Index

Index of Charts
and Lists

A Christian Writer's Manual of Style
was typeset on a Mergenthaler Linotron 202/N.
Main entries are set in 10-point Electra,
and examples in 9-point Optima.
Printed by Patterson Printing
of Benton Harbor, Michigan.